The Classical America Series in Art and Arc

<small>HENRY HOPE REED AND H. STAFFORD BRYANT JR., GENERAL EDITORS</small>

MONOGRAPH OF THE WORK

OF

McKIM, MEAD & WHITE

1879–1915

STUDENT'S EDITION

The Classical America Series in Art and Architecture

Henry Hope Reed and H. Stafford Bryant, Jr., General Editors

Forthcoming with the Architectural Book Publishing Company:
The Student's Edition of Paul Letarouilly's Buildings of Renaissance Rome,
edited by John Barrington Bayley

With W. W. Norton & Company:

The Architecture of Humanism by Geoffrey Scott
The Decoration of Houses by Edith Wharton and Ogden Codman, Jr.
The Classic Point of View by Kenyon Cox
*Fragments from Greek and Roman Architecture: The Classical
America Edition of Hector d'Espouy's Plates*
The Golden City by Henry Hope Reed
Guide to the Decoration of the Library of Congress by Herbert Small
*Monumental Classic Architecture in Great Britain and Ireland in
the XVIIIth and XIXth Centuries* by Albert E. Richardson
Classical America IV, edited by William A. Coles

Classical America is the society founded to encourage the classical tradition
in the arts of the United States.

The Classical America Series in Art and Architecture

MONOGRAPH OF THE WORK
OF
McKIM, MEAD & WHITE
1879–1915

STUDENT'S EDITION

With an Introduction by Allan Greenberg
and Biographical Notes by Michael George

ARCHITECTURAL BOOK PUBLISHING COMPANY

Stamford, Connecticut, 06903

ACKNOWLEDGEMENT

This student edition of the Monograph of McKim, Mead & White, with the enlightening introductions of Allan Greenberg and Michael J. George, is a significant contribution by Classical America towards its goal of reviving an appreciation and understanding of the classical tradition in architecture, which has been an integral and important aspect of America's esthetic heritage.

At the turn of the century, and subsequently, McKim, Mead & White firmly established the classical tradition with many of America's most important buildings. Although, for a time, the principles which guided the firm have not been pursued, nevertheless, in the longer sweep of history the present turning to the classical is an extension of McKim, Mead & White's vision—a natural and welcome circumstance.

The Arthur Ross Foundation is pleased to participate in the publication of this important book.

ARTHUR ROSS

Copyright © 1981, 1925 by Architectural Book
Publishing Co., Inc.

Second printing, November, 1991

Library of Congress Cataloging in Publication Data

McKim, Mead & White.
Monograph of the work of McKim, Mead & White, 1879–1915.
(The Classical America series in art and architecture)
Bibliography: p.
1. McKim, Mead & White. 2. Architecture, Modern—19th
century—United States. 3. Architecture, Modern—20th
century—United States. I. Title. II. Series: Classical
America series in art and architecture.
NA737.M4A4 1981   720'.92'2   81-3455
AACR2
ISBN 0-8038-6775-1

Published simultaneously in Canada by Saunders of Toronto, Ltd., Don Mills, Ontario

Printed in the United States of America

CONTENTS

Elevation of a Farmhouse in Greenwich, Connecticut, whose design was inspired by American colonial and federal period architecture (*architect, Allan Greenberg*)

INTRODUCTION

by ALLAN GREENBERG, Director, Classical America

On board I soon found, to my surprise, that the ordinary American man or woman—whom I there met knew not only the names of the architects in their towns and their chief buildings, but also where in the States I should find, say, the latest work of Messrs. McKim, Mead and White, or of Carrère and Hastings.[1]

THE LEGACY OF Charles Follen McKim, Stanford White, and William Rutherford Mead is so vast that at this point in time both the outer boundaries of its influence and the inner characteristics of the architecture are only barely discernible to anyone interested in their work. As architects of some of the most important buildings in the history of American architecture, the work of the office of McKim, Mead & White reached a level of quality that has not been equalled by any large office before or since.

The breadth of their work between 1879 and 1915 spanned virtually every type of building: McKim, Mead & White's commissions include houses, mansions, casinos, hotels, row houses, apartment buildings, libraries, hospitals, museums, exhibition and entertainment buildings, and churches, university and civic buildings. Among their finest creations are the Morgan Library, Municipal Building, University Club and Pennsylvania Railroad Station, sadly demolished—all in New York. Their work also includes the Boston Public Library, the renovation of, and additions to, the Rotunda at the University of Virginia, the Metropolitan Museum of Art, and the White House, and the complexes of buildings for the campuses of Columbia University, the Bronx Campus of New York University, now the Bronx Community Col-

lege, and the Army War College at Fort McNair in the District of Columbia.

The office assisted Daniel Burnham in the creation of the World's Columbian Exposition of 1893 in Chicago. McKim, Burnham, Augustus Saint Gaudens, the sculptor, and Frederick Law Olmsted, Jr., prepared the McMillan Commission Report of 1902 on the future growth and development of the District of Columbia. This study remains among the most influential and comprehensive physical planning studies which were ever executed for major cities. McKim himself worked on the crucial Mall area, making recommendations which were instrumental in creating the Mall with which we are all so familiar today.

McKim virtually redirected the course of American architecture. He had a vision of a "Golden City Beautiful" which grew out of his love of the masterpieces of ancient Roman, Italian Renaissance and colonial and federal American architecture; this vision sweeps aside the remnants of Victorian and Richardsonian influence and dulls the lustre, in the United States, of French Architecture. McKim and White are, to a large degree, responsible for the strong revival of interest in 17th and 18th century American architecture, the impact of which still remains potent. Their dream of an American architecture of urbanity, beauty and grace frequently provided the impetus for the creation of that core of classical buildings which so often forms the most beautiful parts of towns and cities all over the United States. Most of these groups of buildings and related open spaces were realised by the succeeding generation of architects. There was widespread public interest in the work of McKim, Mead & White which was fundamental to the extraordinary success of the office and the perpetuation of its legacy. The name McKim, Mead & White became a household word in circles concerned about architecture, civic design and improvement of the quality of life in urban America.

McKim and White believed painting and sculpture to be an integral part of architecture and actively commissioned work from both painters and sculptors to adorn their buildings. To promote this objective, McKim spearheaded the drive to create the American Academy in Rome. Here, he hoped, architecture, painting and sculpture could be studied together in harmony at the very fountainhead of western art. Elected president of the American Institute of Architects in 1902, McKim worked arduously to strengthen the prestige of the profession and to improve the quality of architectural education.

Perhaps the most important legacy of the office was the group of distinguished architects of the succeeding generation who were trained in the firm's drafting rooms. These include some of the most outstanding practitioners, such as John Mervyn Carrère, Thomas Hastings, Henry Bacon, H. van Buren Magonigle, Edward Palmer York, Philip Sawyer, Cass Gilbert, John Mead Howells and Egerton Swartwout, as well as the teacher A. D. F. Hamlin and the art critic Royal Cortissoz.

The recent resurgence of interest in the work of McKim, Mead & White is heartening. One of the most unfortunate trends in architectural history since World War II is the neglect of their buildings as well as those of the next generation of classical architects including such important offices as Bakewell & Brown, Delano & Aldrich, York & Sawyer, John Russell Pope, Paul P. Cret, Henry Bacon, Philip Trammell Shutze, David Adler, and Mott B. Schmidt. During this period, while the mainstream has centered on Modernism, interest in classical architecture has been kept alive by a diverse coalition of groups, such as Classical America and the New York City Landmarks Conservancy, which supported its promotion and preservation. The most important source of support for classical architecture, though, is the general public whose love for the beautiful traditional buildings of America remains undiminished and whose activities brought into being the preservation movement.

The re-issue of this Student's Edition of the Monograph of the Work of McKim, Mead & White is a part of the larger process of reassessment of architecture and architectural history which is now underway. This movement will eventually address the critically important issue of re-evaluating the work and influence of McKim, Mead & White. However, the republishing of this book of their architectural drawings provides occasion to explore the uses for which it was originally intended and which are now, largely, forgotten. This loss of memory grows out of the Modernist's preoccupation with novelty of form and expression of the "genius" latent in each individual architect. These attitudes are, of course, antithetical to classical design.

The design of classical buildings is similar to the workings of the law. In architecture, it is great buildings and complexes of buildings that are used to provide material to develop case studies from which precedent is developed. These great buildings are documented by means of measured drawings, which may be supplemented by photographs or perspective sketches. A considerable number of buildings covering all periods of architectural history have been so documented, though not all have been published.

These books fall into two basic types. One type deals with whole buildings and may document single structures such as the Palazzo Massimo[2] or Petit Trianon[3], a complex of buildings such as the Vatican[4], building types such as Wren's London Churches[5], or the work of an individual architect or office, such as the monograph of McKim, Mead & White's work.[6] The purpose of these studies is to establish both the functional and aesthetic bases of the building's design. The second type of book explores in more detail the articulation of the classical orders and their related mouldings and decorative elements[7]. In the 19th and 20th centuries, under the influence of the Ecole des Beaux Arts, the subject matter of this group of books was expanded to include the planning of buildings based on axes.[8]

The process of collecting data on buildings to use to establish case studies on precedent goes back to antiquity. In his book, the Roman architect Vitruvius refers to the work of Greek architects; during the Dark and Middle Ages, plans of churches, cathedrals, monasteries, and other building types were formalized based on precedent. Master builders like Vuillard d'Honnecourt recorded interesting aspects of such buildings. The Renaissance formalized the process of studying the past by converting it into a humanist discipline; architects devoted considerable effort to documenting the physical remains of ancient Rome. Some of this

Drawing of a Roman Corinthian capital from Palladio's *Four Books of Architecture,* Isaac Ware trans. Bk. 4, pl. 9, Dover Publications.

work, like Palladio's sketches and measured drawings, continues to be immensely important. Visitors to Italy from north of the Alps began to supplement the documentation of antiquity by studies and measurement of the works of Renaissance and Baroque masters.

The use of precedent in architectural design has numerous functions, many of which are today misunderstood or neglected. The primary function of precedent is to develop case studies which can be used to form a canon and establish norms. This provides both practitioner and client with a range of principles and ideas from which to develop architectural designs. These include systems of organization for plan, elevation and massing, as well as examples of detailing of orders, and selecting mouldings and decorative motifs so as to properly solve function and express meaning and decorum in an appropriate and beautiful manner.

It is important to understand that the availability

of a canon is not a prescription for copying. For the architect of the Renaissance, for example, the consideration of precedent provided the opportunity to rationally consider and select sources. In this way an architect could display individuality and "surpass the past while using the forms the past could give him."[9] They called the process *imitation.* To merely copy was considered an abdication of responsibility. This position is clearly stated by Petrarch who in *Le Familiari* suggested that imitation should aim towards the sort of similarity as exists between father and son, rather than exactness or literalness. Petrarch spoke of the shadow and *air* in the face and eyes that makes the son resemble the father, and his advice to the artist is to seek another man's "quality and tone". (This passage is well translated by the art historian E. M. Gombrich in *Norm and Form.*) The application to architecture seems plain enough.[10]

In this same vein, Aretino writes of Giulio Romano's work as "anciently modern and modernly ancient."[11]

This principle is clearly demonstrated by the way in which architects worked at design problems over the drawing-board. It is crucial to grasp that the canon itself is little more than a general principle. The Doric cornice consists of a cymatium, corona, dentils, bed mould, frieze of triglyph and metope, taenia and fascia, yet the same combination of forms is treated differently by Sir Edwin Lutyens, Palladio and Stanford White. While we talk, glibly, of the Doric order, the architect drawing a Doric cornice, capital, or column has to ask, "What Doric? Whose variation?" For close study reveals that the ancient Greek architects almost always developed a subtle new variation for each project, as illustrated on the following pages.

During Roman antiquity and the Renaissance, architects continued this tradition. Even within the very limited framework of the Doric capital, the range of formal *speculation* by architects over three thousand years is extraordinary. The canon was no more constricting or inhibiting to architects like Iktinos, Apollodorus, Bramante, François Mansart or Jefferson than was the English language or sonnet form to Shakespeare, Pope, Keats or Stevens.

This presents us with the following irony: *While the canon limits the forms which can be used to a given language, the result is an accumulation of such rich formal variation that when the material is absorbed into case studies, the architect has virtually an unlimited choice.* Seen in this context, the canon is a liberating tool. As far back as Vitruvius architects dreamt of transforming architecture from mere craft into a liberal art.[12] From the Renaissance until the 1920's in Europe, and the 1940's in the United States, the principles of imitation facilitated this transformation. In the United States, the result was the creation of architecture departments in our great universities, starting at the Massachusetts Institute of Technology.

The uses of the principles of imitation go far beyond form and aesthetics. *Commodity, firmness and delight* all rely on precedent. *Commodity* is established by the use of the typological solutions which

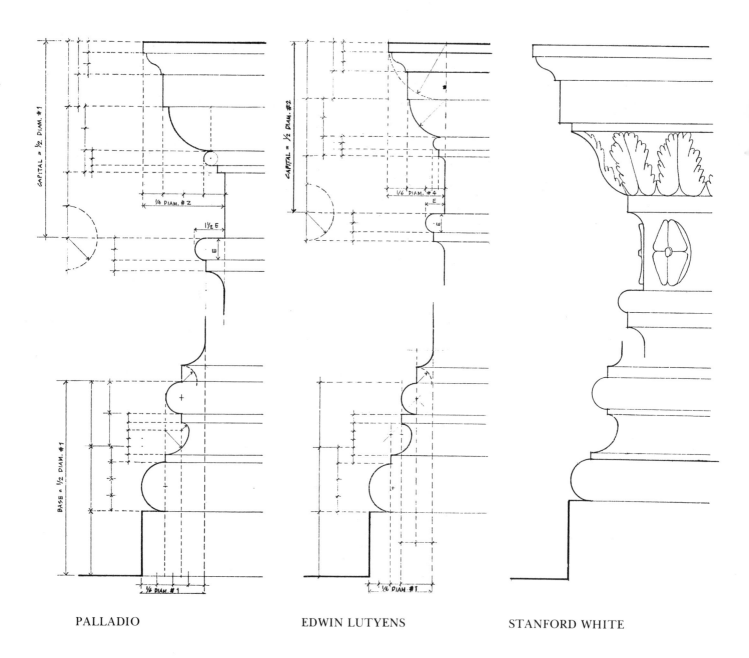

PALLADIO   EDWIN LUTYENS   STANFORD WHITE

The Doric order designed by Palladio, Edwin Landseer Lutyens and Stanford White. Lutyens and White base their designs on Palladio but alter the profile of the mouldings. At the Midland Bank at Poultney in London, Lutyens's column supports five floors and the torus, scotia and echinus are modified to impart a greater sense of compression. White's column is part of a decorative screen at the carriage entrance to the Metropolitan Club in New York. His base is higher and the Doric echinus is replaced by a cyma decorated with leaves which offsets any sense of structural support. This is reinforced by the slight enlargement of the mouldings, which imparts a sense of vertical movement.

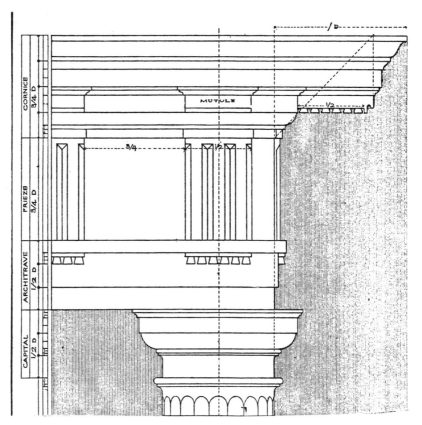

cymatium

corona

mutules

bedmould

metope

triglyphs

taenia
fascias

abacus

echinus

neckline

astragal

Drawing of a section through a typical Doric capital and cornice as drawn by William R. Ware, from his handbook, *The American Vignola*, Classical America Series in Art and Architecture, W. W. Norton & Company.

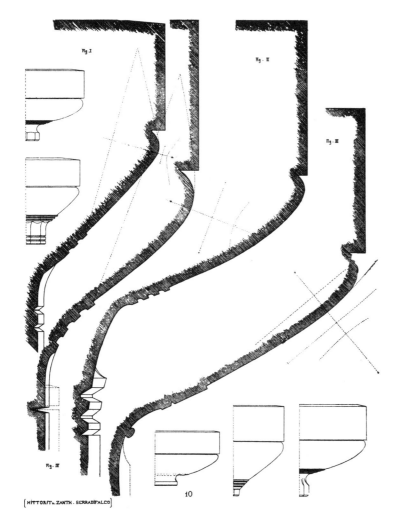

Doric capitals from a selection of Greek Temples showing the variation of capital design. Each curve drastically affects the perception, both visually and physically, of the column and its relation to the lintel, load and roof of the building. From Constantin Uhde's, *The Architectural Forms of Classic Ages . . .* Revised by R. Phene Spiers (Berlin, 1909)

are continuously adjusted to suit changing social, political, religious or functional needs. Without such a system of building types, architects are forced to "re-invent the wheel" with each new commission as the experience of the past is not available in codified form. *Firmness* relies on precedent to establish criteria for both structural safety and sound construction. *Delight* is based on the architect's ability to master the canon of classical architecture. In this way, *design* is married to scholarship through the intelligent use of the past. (The terms *commodity, firmness* and *delight* are generally regarded as the invention of Sir Henry Wotton, the English diplomat, man of letters, and art connoisseur of the late Tudor and early Stuart periods.)

Since 1950, architects have been educated to disdain using precedent of any sort. For this reason, the great corpus of classical and Gothic design was disparagingly designated as mere copying—except, perhaps, for the Gothic expression of structure. Even functional precedent was not formulated as each architect reserved the right to interpret design problems in his or her own special way. The result is arbitrary functional criteria, shoddy construction techniques, and aesthetic problems which are hardly defined, as each architect is preoccupied with attempting to invent a new formal system. Despite obvious public disenchantment with many recent buildings, this point of view still persists in many schools of architecture.

Without a canon, the average practitioner is left with the impossible task of developing his or her own formal system and functional solutions. This is an almost insurmountable problem, because each generation produces only a few truly great designers. We forget that Michelangelo's stupendous genius was forged using the classical language of architecture and that even his great mind did not invent a new language of architecture but was content to expand, transform, and extend a tradition. The result today of the disdain of precedent is a cult of fashion and novelty based on surreptitious copying. It is an indisputable fact that the vast majority of practitioners and students cannot invent new forms and must rely on others for their ideas. Unfortunately, architectural journals have replaced scholarship and study of precedent with fashions and fads as sources of ideas in the search for competence and beauty.

The elements of classical architecture provide a sophisticated language of form and meaning whose syntax and grammar have been refined for over 3,000 years. Its various aspects are so complex and integrated that it is difficult to separate the components of function, construction, and aesthetics. Elements such as cornices, columns, and wainscots, for example, may be decorative, *functional*, or serve as elements of construction. This tripartite aspect cannot be reduced to a single use, such as columns which merely support or wainscoting whose only purpose is to reduce maintenance cost, without destroying the very nature of the language.

The application of precedent presents the architect at the drawing board with a variety of challenges. It enables a great architect to master the canon so completely that its boundaries may be extended and new precedent established. These new ideas may be absorbed into the canon, or, alternatively, remain an isolated *tour de force* which other architects do not care, or dare, to emulate. The *double order* and *serliana* are inventions which have been absorbed into the canon. The Wren London church is an example of a building type whose influence continues to be felt today in the United States. On the other hand, many of the brilliant designs for mouldings and combinations of mouldings invented by Borromini have not been further developed by other architects.

The more common use of precedent is to enable a practitioner of average competence to produce good buildings. Today, our preoccupation with the individual architect's expressive powers and novelty of form in new building ignores the critical importance of simple background buildings. The row houses, for example, is the basic building block of the great Georgian streets and squares of London, Edinburgh, Boston, Philadelphia, and New York. Countless such background building types serving residential, commercial, and industrial purposes line the streets of towns and cities in Italy, France, England, Scandinavia and the United States. Their quality may vary, but they form the bulk of the built environment and, as such, the setting for the more important religious, civic, and public buildings. The formidable design challenge presented by these buildings is suggested by the splendid Percy Pyne house (plate 129) by McKim and 130 East 80th Street, New York, by Mott B. Schmidt. These are examples of row houses whose superb designs transcend the norm.

Having a canon to refer to has enabled generations of architects to produce competent buildings which solve, in a simple, straightforward way, urbanistic, functional, and aesthetic problems. The canon assists the average practitioner to solve complex planning problems, use sound construction techniques, and produce solid buildings that enhance the environment. It is only recently that, for the first time in the history of architecture, society has been *unable* to assume that architects can design such buildings and precincts.

By collecting the experience of the past and formulating it into a canon based on case studies, classical architecture becomes a liberating design tool. It frees the architect from the superhuman task of inventing new sets of forms, functional solutions, and construction systems. By following the example of the great architects of the past, the designer is able to produce beautiful buildings which express the aspirations of the institution they house.

The best buildings of McKim, Mead & White, some of the finest and most provocative classical designs in American architecture, are presented in this volume by plan, elevation, and details. The information gleaned by studying these drawings can be used to develop case studies of building types, from both functional and aesthetic points of view, and to facilitate detailed consideration of the articulation of the Orders and mouldings. Study of these drawings raises questions in the student's mind: Why were the different plans, architectural forms, and sets of relationships used? How are various effects of shade, shadow, and sunlit surfaces achieved? And, finally, what is the source of form, meaning, and idea? The knowledge gained by answering these questions can be expanded by other studies, and eventually applied to work on the drawing board.

This process can be seen at work in the buildings designed by McKim, Mead & White. One of McKim's greatest buildings is the Boston Public Library (plate 23). Brief study of the elevation of this building indicates its two-fold source in Labrouste's Bibliothèque Sainte Geneviève in Paris and Alberti's San Francesco in Rimini.[13] The principle of a rusticated first floor with small windows, central entrance and a second floor with arcades stretched across the front, behind which is a main reading room, is rooted in Labrouste. The detail of the arcade is based on the Rimini building. However, the development of both building and detail by McKim is quite different from the precedents. Notice the Boston Public Library's bold and richly modelled cornice, its sculptural string courses at plinth and at second floor levels, and the detailing of the spring point of the arches. Labrouste's building is the product of a different sensibility. The string course at the second floor level is a projecting shelf; mouldings are spartan and the simple step-backs at the plinth disdain use of any modelling. Perhaps the difference can best be

seen in the upper portion of the building where McKim increases the area devoted to windows and makes the cornice larger and more elaborate.

The richly modelled string courses and window frames are derived from the High Renaissance in Rome, Rimini, and Venice. Note McKim's triple arch entrance and how different from Labrouste are his loggia, staircase, iron work and articulation of the second floor reading rooms. The interior courtyard was probably inspired by the exquisite cortiles at the Ducal Palace at Urbino of 1444 designed by Luciano Laurana and the Palazzo della Cancelleria, Rome 1486–96. The scale of McKim's building is grander and the upper portions lack pilasters, but the contrast between brick and stone, use of arched loggia, and closed upper floors are

Detail of the elevation and section of the Bibliothèque Sainte Geneviève in Paris designed by Henri Labrouste. This building provided one precedent for the design of the Boston Public Library. (*Drawing by Allan Greenberg*)

Victory Leading General Sherman, sculptor, Augustus Saint-Gaudens; architect, Charles Follen McKim. This beautiful statue is at the corner of Fifth Avenue and 59th Street in New York. (*Photo, Allan Greenberg*)

based on the Italian masterpieces. Differences abound between the library and its prototypes. A study of both similarities and differences is again richly rewarding.

The great campus at Columbia University was inspired by the example of the 1893 World's Columbian Exposition at Chicago and the Nénot design for the Sorbonne in Paris.[14] The development of the Pantheon ideal from Ancient Rome, via Jefferson, to the Low Library is a marvelous challenge to the appreciation of the genius of the architects of all three buildings. The layout at Columbia may also have grown out of Jefferson's plan for the University of Virginia at Charlottesville. Columbia,

in turn, inspired Cass Gilbert's layout for the University of Minnesota at Minneapolis.

McKim, Mead & White revitalized the design of the town house with such beautiful structures as the Nickerson and Pyne houses. Study of these designs will provide ample rewards for designer and student. At a smaller scale, the brilliant collaboration between sculptors like Augustus Saint-Gaudens, Frederick MacMonnies, Stanford White and McKim should be discussed. Stanford White and Augustus Saint-Gaudens designed the innovative memorial to Admiral Farragut where the unity of form of sculpture, typography, and architecture describes the shared vision of these two men.

Horse Tamers, sculptor, Frederick MacMonnies; architect, Stanford White. This splendid evocation of man attempting to restrain and control the forces of nature stands at one of the entrances to Prospect Park, Brooklyn. (*Photo, Allan Greenberg*)

McKim and Saint-Gaudens collaborated on the great Shaw Memorial on the Boston Common. However, their finest work, also commemorating the Civil War, is the statue of Victory leading General Sherman, situated at the southeast corner of Central Park. McKim's design for the base is the equal of the best equestrian statue bases in Europe.

It is a fascinating exercise to compare this base with the exquisitely detailed base by White for MacMonnies's rearing horses at one of the entrances to Prospect Park. Both designs were inspired by Michelangelo's base for the equestrian statue of Marcus Aurelius on the Capitoline in Rome. All three bases use similar mouldings, profiles, and proportions. McKim's is executed in red

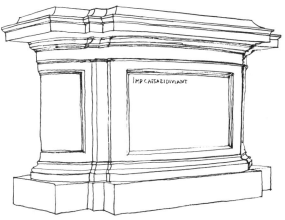

Base by Michelangelo for the equestrian statue of Marcus Aurelius which stands on the Capitoline in Rome.

Palazzo Strozzi in Florence, which was one of the precedents for the University Club. *Photograph, courtesy, American Academy, Rome.*

of piers. The use of awning, iron balcony and a splendidly scaled cornice all add a special touch to the McKim work.

The interior plan is based on the idea of an enclosed Renaissance cortile, which is repeated on several of the floors and receives direct light through windows on the rear wall which face a second open courtyard space. The cornice designs of the University Club and Palazzo Strozzi should be compared. The latter building is 104′6″ high and has a 12′8″ cornice; the former is 125′ high with a 14′ cornice. The crucial detail is the smaller frieze at the University Club, which has the effect of increasing the scale of the upper portion of the cornice. The mouldings of the two cornices should have similar profiles, but the richer modelling and increased scale of the elements in the New York building clearly differentiate it from the Renaissance prototype. Exercises like this could be continued indefinitely and should be expanded to include the noble interiors with their ambitious decorative program.

One of McKim, Mead & White's most important buildings is the Municipal Building in New York. This thirty-story skyscraper has a triumphal arch

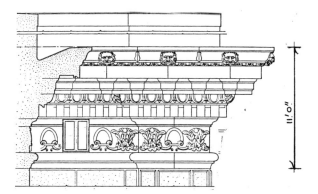

Comparative sections through the cornices of the University Club (above) and the Palazzo Strozzi (below). Source for the University Club, plate 44. (*Drawing, Allan Greenberg*)

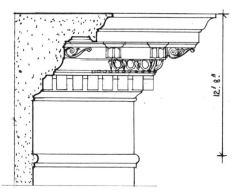

granite, which accounts for the flatter projections and the absence of deep undercutting. The different sensibilities of the designers can be easily assessed by comparing White's delicacy of the Roman detail, McKim's powerful architectonic vision and the Michelangelo expression of sculptural force in stone. None is "original," for even the Marcus Aurelius base was derived from earlier Renaissance and Roman precedent.

McKim's University Club (plate 42) and White's Century Association (plate 34) are, architecturally speaking, the greatest designs for New York clubs. McKim's inspiration was the Florentine Palazzos Ricardi and Strozzi. Detailed comparison of these buildings yields fascinating results. With obvious gusto, McKim displays the intervening floors, which are frequently hidden on the main elevation of Renaissance buildings and only revealed at the side or rear elevations. The smaller windows and alternating sculptural plaques at the second and fourth floor levels introduce a syncopated rhythm and the corners are reinforced by the suggestion in the center of a screen at its base which provides the surrounding civic precinct with a monumental gateway. The body of the building, which contains 22 floors of offices, rises majestically above the base. Its exterior is articulated by chaste modelling, which expresses structure, defines the vertical runs of windows and controls shadow and highlight. This mass is capped by a three-story–high Corinthian Order and a bold cornice, both of which are penetrated by windows and crowned by sculpture. The central section of the building is extended eight or nine floors above the main mass and is topped by a circular spire and statue.

The building is one of the grandest expressions of the skyscraper in the United States. The classical language of architecture enabled McKim, Mead & White to create a structure which is readily experienced by eye, mind and body through the pro-cess of empathy described by Geoffrey Scott in *The Architecture of Humanism.* The building's impact on its urban setting is brilliant. The tower speaks to the horizon, the base screen wall to the street, and the office floors create a wall to define the northeast corner of the government precinct and, most important of all, the beautiful Corinthian Order of the screen wall sets the scale for the later United States Courthouse and the New York County Courthouse to the north as well as relating to the older "Tweed" Courthouse to the west. It is also a functional and efficient office building. This wonderful structure, like so many others in the book, remains a potent guide into the future:

The path lies in darkness, but as the light dawns behind, it will be seen that great deeds have been done along the way.[15]

Municipal Building, 1908, in New York, designed by McKim, Mead & White, (see plates 100 and 101), stands to the east (right) of City Hall, "Tweed" Courthouse and Hall of Records. (*Photograph, Joseph C. Farber, courtesy H. H. Reed*

NOTES

1. C. H. Reilly, *"The Modern Renaissance in American Architecture."* Royal Institute of British Architects' Journal, June 25, 1910, p. 630.
2. T. F. Suys et L. P. Haudebourt, *Palais Massimi à Rome,* Paris: Librairie Des Arts Décoratifs, 1908.
3. Leon Deshaers, *Le Petit Trianon, architecture-decoration-ameublement,* Paris: Librairie Des Arts Décoratifs, 1908.
4. Paul-Marie Letarouilly, *Le Vatican et la Basilique de Saint Pierre de Rome,* Paris: A. Morel et Cie, 1882.
5. John Clayton, *The Dimensions, plans and elevations of the Parochial Churches of Sir Christopher Wren, Erected in the Cities of London and Westminister,* London: Longman, Brown, Green and Longman, 1848–9.
6. *Monograph of the Works of McKim, Mead & White, 1879–1915,* New York: Architectural Book Publishing Co., 1915.
7. Antoine Desgodets, *Les Edifices Antiques de Rome,* Rome: V. Poggioli, 1822
8. Nathaniel C. Curtis: *Architectural Composition,* Cleveland: J. H. Jansen, 1923
9. David Cast, *Liberty: Honor: Virtue: Comment on the Position of the Visual Arts in the Renaissance,* Yale Italian Studies, Fall 1977, p. 375.
10. Francesca Petrarca, *Le familiari,* quoted on p. 122 in E. H. Gombrich, *Norm and Form,* London: Phaidon Press, 1966, p. 81.
11. Pietro Aretino, *Il secondo libro delle lettere,* quoted in E. H. Gombrich, ibid. p. 127.
12. Frank E. Brown, *Vitruvius and the Liberal Art of Architecture,* Bucknell Review, 1962, pp. 99–107.
13. William H. Jordy, *American Buildings and Their Architects, Progressive and Academic Ideals at the Turn of the Twentieth Century,* Garden City: Doubleday and Co., 1972, pp. 314–375. This superb analysis of the Boston Public Library has been the basis of my own observations.
14. Francesco Passanti, *The Design of Columbia in the 1890's, McKim and His Client,* Journal of the Society of Architectural Historians, no. II, 1977. pp. 69–84.
15. Fiske Kimball, *American Architecture,* Indianapolis and New York: Bobbs-Merrill Co. 1928, p. 228.

BIOGRAPHICAL NOTES
ON THE MEN OF McKIM, MEAD & WHITE

BY MICHAEL GEORGE, DIRECTOR, CLASSICAL AMERICA

BERT FENNER

Bert Leslie Fenner was born in Rochester, N.Y. in 1869, the son of Edward Fenner and Margaret Taylor Fenner. He attended the University of Rochester and studied architecture at the Massachusetts Institute of Technology in the years 1890–91. Following graduation, Fenner worked briefly in Rochester but then, in the fall of 1891, took a job with McKim, Mead & White as a draftsman. In 1906 he was named a partner in the firm. Fenner contributed to the designs of several buildings, including the main Post Office building in New York City (1912), the Municipal Building in New York (1912), the Minneapolis Museum of Fine Arts (1913), the Hotel Pennsylvania in New York, which is now the Hotel Statler Hilton (1918), and the Nashville (Tennessee) War Memorial (1923).

Fenner's study on the heights of structures was the basis in drafting the first comprehensive zoning law in the United States, the New York city zoning ordinance of 1916. In 1918, Fenner served as general manager of the United States Housing Commission. He was president of the American Institute of Architects from 1919 to 1920.

Fenner took an interest in the relations between architect, builders and the trade unions. He sought to reconcile the groups. He sought a better training system for apprentices. He was able to bring the architects and the trade unions together to study apprentice training. In 1922, Fenner served as chairman of a joint committee of the American Institute of Architects (AIA) and the Building Trades Employees Association, which investigated poor working conditions and labor-management controversies in the building trades. In addition, Fenner succeeded in getting the American Institute of Architects, contractors and trade unions to sponsor a study of the basic apprentice training system. Fenner also sought to have fledgling workers as well trained as the veterans.

Fenner married the former Louise McKittrick in 1896. He died of heat stroke in 1926 and is buried in Sleepy Hollow Cemetery, Tarrytown, N.Y.

WILLIAM MITCHELL KENDALL

William Mitchell Kendall was born in 1856, the son of Joshua and Phoebe (Mitchell) Kendall. The elder Kendall was a scholar of Dante. The younger Kendall attended Harvard College and studied architecture at the Massachusetts Institute of Technology. After beginning work in the office of McKim, Mead and White in 1882, Kendall was named a partner in the firm in 1906.

Kendall worked on several projects including the Butler Art Gallery in Youngstown, Ohio (1912), the Municipal Building in New York City (1912), the Savoy Plaza Hotel in New York City (1928), the Arlington Memorial Bridge in Washington, D.C. (1932), the Plymouth Rock Portico in Plymouth, Mass. (1921), and the main Post Office building in New York City (1913). The often quoted inscription on the frieze of the Post Office building: "Neither snow, nor rain, nor heat, nor gloom of night, stays these couriers from the swift completion of their appointed rounds" was the inspiration of the architects of the building and not their client. The quotation was taken from Herodotus and it seemed appropriate for the frieze, which is nearly two blocks long. It has become the unofficial motto of the Post Office.

In 1929, Kendall was appointed to a United States Commission on planning and designing cemeteries for the American war dead in France and Italy. Kendall lived to the age of 85. He died in Bar Harbor, Maine, in 1941.

CHARLES FOLLEN McKIM

Charles Follen McKim was born in Chester County, Pennsylvania in 1847. His parents, James Miller McKim and Sarah Speakman McKim, were Quakers and Abolitionists. William Lloyd Garrison, the great American anti-slavery leader was a relative by marriage. When John Brown was executed, Mrs. McKim assisted the widow in claiming the body.

Charles McKim was the second of two children. He was named after Karl Follen, the first professor of German at Harvard, who later would lose his post because of his abolitionist sympathies. Young Charles McKim attended schools in Perth Amboy, New Jersey and Philadelphia. He entered the Lawrence Scientific School at Harvard in 1866 with the intent to study mining engineering. McKim took to athletics at Harvard and made the varsity baseball team. Yet he stayed at Harvard only one year. Instead, McKim turned to the study of architecture. He entered the Ecole des Beaux Arts in 1867, enrolling in the atelier of Honoré Daumet. Daumet was the winner of the Prix de Rome in 1855, architect of the Château de Chantilly and a close friend of Hector d'Espouy, author of *Fragments of Greek and Roman Architecture,* a book reprinted by W. W. Norton & Company, Inc. in the Classical America Series in Art and Architecture. While abroad, McKim traveled to Northern Italy, Austria, Germany, and England. While McKim failed to win prizes during his time at the Ecole, he was an expert draftsman. (He could, incidentally, write and draw with either hand, and he could also write backwards.) McKim remained at the Ecole until 1870 and the outbreak of the Franco-Prussian War, when he returned home.

McKim settled in New York City. He took a job with the architectural office of Charles Gambrill and Henry H. Richardson. His starting salary was eight dollars per week. He stayed with the firm two years. During that time McKim was involved in the preliminary drawing for Richardson's project of Trinity Church in Boston. McKim began his own practice after leaving Gambrill and Richardson. He rented space in the same building and began getting commissions to design houses for friends. It is a poignant note that McKim's place at Gambrill and Richardson was taken by a 19-year-old red-headed youth named Stanford White.

In 1878, McKim formed a partnership with William B. Bigelow, his brother-in-law, and William Rutherford Mead. The following year Bigelow left the firm and Stanford White replaced him. Thus the firm McKim, Mead & White was born.

In 1878, McKim, Mead and White had taken their "celebrated trip to New England," as they called it, for the purpose of seeing and measuring examples of Colonial and Federal architecture.

McKim did important work on such major building projects as: The Villard Houses (1882), which are now built into Helmsley Palace Hotel; the Boston Public Library (1887), the 1893 Chicago World's Columbian Exposition, the Agriculture Building at the 1893 Chicago World's Fair, the Columbia University campus (1897), Symphony Hall in Boston (1900), alterations to the White House (1902), the Pierpont Morgan Library (1906), Pennsylvania Station in New York City (1904), and the University Club in New York (1897).

McKim served on the McMillan Commission, the body which redrafted the plan of Washington D.C. The report of the Commission led to the formal design of the Mall and the selection of sites for several major federal monuments, including the Lincoln Memorial and the Arlington Memorial Bridge.

McKim established the American Academy in Rome, where American students could study the classical heritage. He raised money for the building, secured a federal charter for the institution and was the first president of the Academy. McKim provided traveling scholarships so that architecture students in this country could travel abroad and see the examples of great buildings there.

McKim won abundant honors. He was elected President of the American Institute of Architects in 1902. He received the Gold Medal of the Royal Institute of British architects in 1903 and honorary degrees from Harvard (1890), Bowdoin College (1894), Columbia University (1904), and the University of Pennsylvania (1909) and was awarded the Gold Medal of the American Institute of Architects in 1909. He served on the first New York City Art Commission in the 1890's.

McKim retired from the firm in 1908 due to failing health. He died on September 14th, 1909, and is buried in Orange, N.J.

McKim was married twice. The first marriage ended in divorce in 1878. There was one daughter. McKim married Julia Appleton in 1885, who died two years later.

WILLIAM RUTHERFORD MEAD

William Rutherford Mead was born in 1846 in Brattleboro, Vt. He was the son of Larkin Goldsmith Mead, a lawyer, and Mary Jane (Noyes) Mead. William Rutherford Mead was one of nine children. One of his brothers, Larkin, became a noted sculptor, and a sister later married the novelist, William Dean Howells.

Mead attended Norwich University for two years, transferred to Amherst, and graduated in 1867. Mead was fond of saying that it was the sight of the Vermont State Capitol at Montpelier, which led him to architecture.

In 1871, Mead traveled to Florence to join his brother Larkin and to study there. Mead studied at the Accademia di Belle Arte. The following year Mead returned to the United States to attend the Massachusetts Institute of Technology. Mead entered into architectural partnership with Charles F. McKim and William Bigelow in 1878. Bigelow left the firm the following year and Stanford White stepped in.

While Mead is not as well known as McKim or White, he enjoyed great prestige among his colleagues and was very influential in the firm. McKim, Mead & White was a collaborative firm. Each partner contributed to the design of the commissions. Mead jested once that his job in the firm was to keep the other two partners from making fools of themselves. Mead became the head of the American Academy in Rome when McKim died. He held that position until his own death in June 1928.

Mead married the former Olga Kilyeni in November 1884. The couple had no children. Mead is buried in the Protestant Cemetery in Florence, Italy.

STANFORD WHITE

Stanford White was born on November 9, 1853. His parents were Richard Grant White, a critic of music and drama, and Alexina Black (Mease) White. The young White displayed a keen sense of drawing and wanted to become a painter. He turned to architecture on the advice of the architect, John LaFarge.

In 1872, White, at the age of 19, began work at the firm of Gambrill and Richardson in New York. The job became available when Charles McKim left the firm to begin his own practice. By 1878 White had saved enough money to travel abroad and he left for Europe in July of that year. He began his travels with McKim and the sculptor, Augustus Saint-Gaudens. White traveled to France, Holland, Belgium and Northern Italy. During the time White was abroad, the firm of McKim, Mead and Bigelow dissolved. McKim and Mead turned to White, who in the words of McKim "could draw like a house afire." White joined in the new partnership in September 1879.

White's energy was virtually boundless. He collaborated with Saint-Gaudens on several sculptural groups. White did the pedestal in these projects, Saint-Gaudens the statue proper. Among the commissions were: the Admiral Farragut monument (1881), the Peter Cooper monument (1894), the Randall monument (1884)—all in New York City. Also, the Lincoln Monument in Chicago (1887), the Puritan Monument in Springfield, Mass. (1887), and the Shaw monument in Boston (1897). White designed magazine covers for *The Century Magazine* and *Scribners'*.

Among his numerous architectural projects were: Madison Square Garden (1891), The Washington Arch (1889), the Judson Memorial Church (1891), the former Bronx Campus of New York University, which is now the Bronx Community College, and the accompanying Hall of Fame of Great Americans (1901), the Tiffany Building (1906), and the Gorham Building (1906). The essayist John Jay Chapman wrote that Stanford White grasped the spirit of the masters of the Renaissance and brought the living flame of their inspiration across the Atlantic to kindle new fires on these shores.

Stanford White's life and career were ended abruptly in 1906 when he was murdered on the roof of Madison Square Garden during a theatrical performance. He was then 53 years old. He is buried in a cemetery at St. James, Long Island. White had married Bessie Springs Smith in 1884.

McKIM, MEAD & WHITE

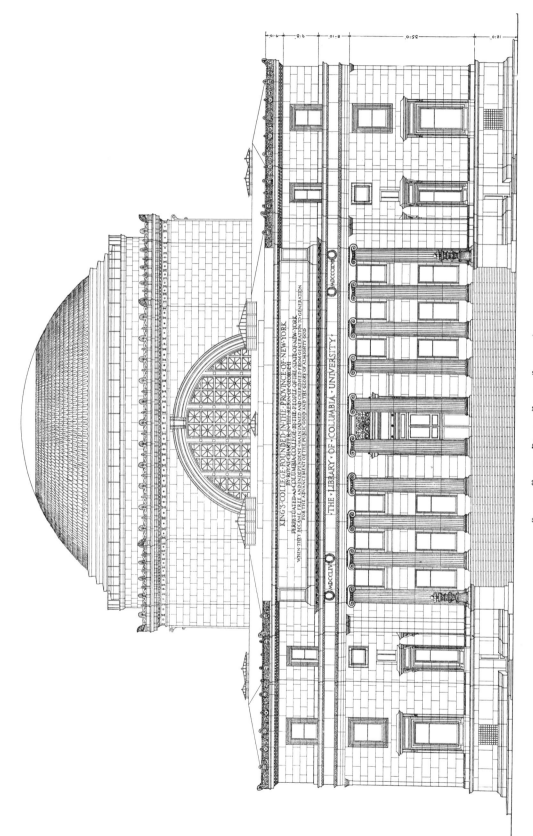

KING'S·COLLEGE·FOUNDED·IN·THE·PROVINCE·OF·NEW·YORK
BY·ROYAL·CHARTER·IN·THE·REIGN·OF·GEORGE·II
PERPETUATED·AS·COLUMBIA·COLLEGE·BY·THE·PEOPLE·OF·THE·STATE·OF·NEW·YORK
WHEN·THEY·BECAME·FREE·AND·INDEPENDENT·MAINTAINED·AND·CHERISHED·FROM·GENERATION·TO·GENERATION
FOR·THE·ADVANCEMENT·OF·THE·PUBLIC·GOOD·AND·THE·GLORY·OF·ALMIGHTY·GOD

·THE··LIBRARY··OF··COLUMBIA··UNIVERSITY·

SCALE

SOUTH ELEVATION

COLUMBIA UNIVERSITY LIBRARY, NEW YORK CITY.
1893

1

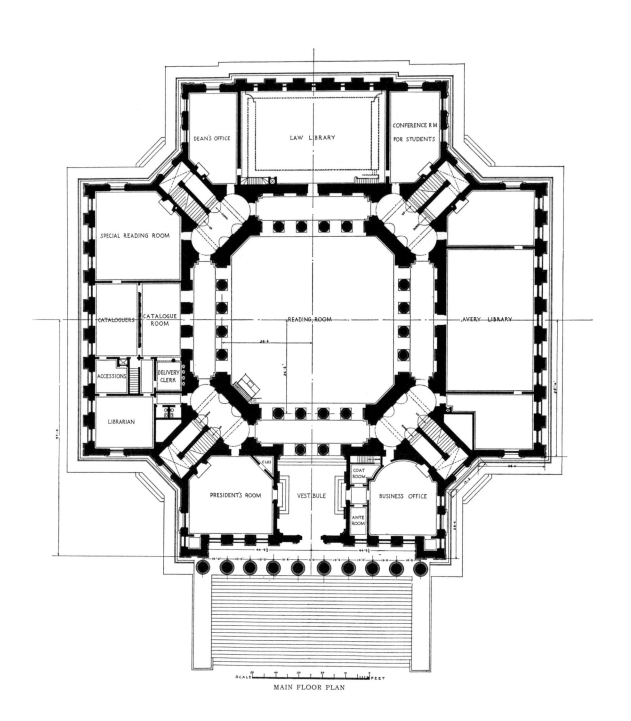

DEAN'S OFFICE

LAW LIBRARY

CONFERENCE R M
FOR STUDENTS

SPECIAL READING ROOM

AVERY LIBRARY

CATALOGUERS

CATALOGUE
ROOM

READING ROOM

ACCESSIONS

DELIVERY
CLERK

LIBRARIAN

CLOS

COAT
ROOM

PRESIDENT'S ROOM

VESTIBULE

BUSINESS OFFICE

ANTE
ROOM

SCALE FEET

MAIN FLOOR PLAN

COLUMBIA UNIVERSITY LIBRARY, NEW YORK CITY.
1893

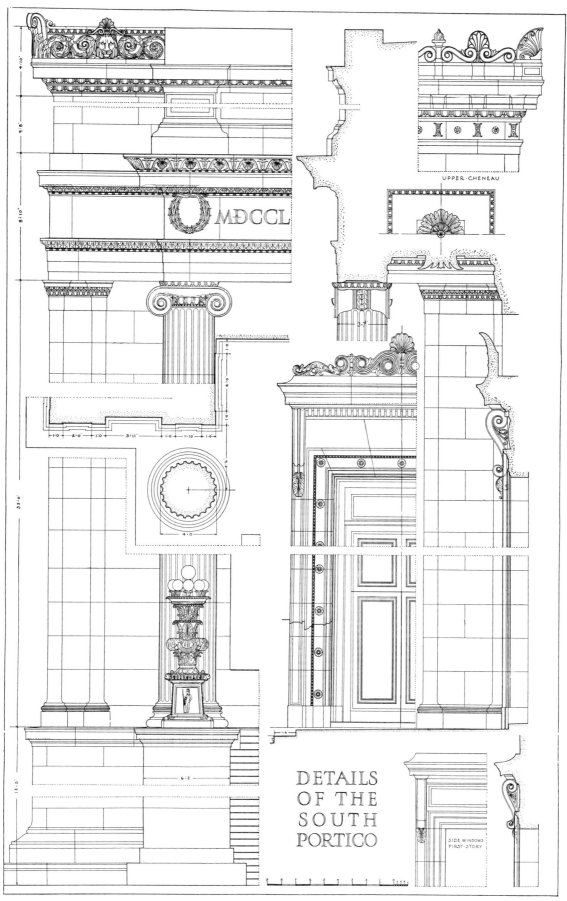

UPPER·CHENEAU

MDCCL

DETAILS
OF THE
SOUTH
PORTICO

SIDE·WINDOWS
FIRST·STORY

COLUMBIA UNIVERSITY LIBRARY, NEW YORK CITY.
1893

ORNAMENT →

LIMESTONE

← ORNAMENT →

ORNAMENT

BRONZE CAPITALS

ASCUTNEY GREEN GRANITE SHAFTS

OPEN

OPEN

CONTINUE

BROWN NUMIDIAN MARBLE

BELGIAN BLACK MARBLE BASE

BRONZE

WROUGHT IRON GATES

CENTRE OF ROOM

FEET 10

5

FLOOR LINE

DETAILS OF READING ROOM
COLUMBIA UNIVERSITY LIBRARY, NEW YORK CITY.
1893

4

· ¾ · INCH · SCALE · DETAIL · AROUND · MAIN · ENTRANCE ·
· PHILOSOPHY · BUILDING · COLUMBIA · UNIVERSITY ·

McKIM, MEAD & WHITE

AUDITORIUM PLAN

PLATFORM

MAIN HALL

LOBBY

SMALL HALL

REFERENCE LIBRARY

FIRST FLOOR PLAN

SMALL HALL

READING ROOM

HALL

BIBLE STUDY

COMMITTEE ROOM

SECRETARY

RECEPTION RM

SCALE

FEET

SOUTH ELEVATION

EARL HALL

SECTION

SCALE

FEET

EARL HALL, COLUMBIA UNIVERSITY, NEW YORK CITY.
1902

6

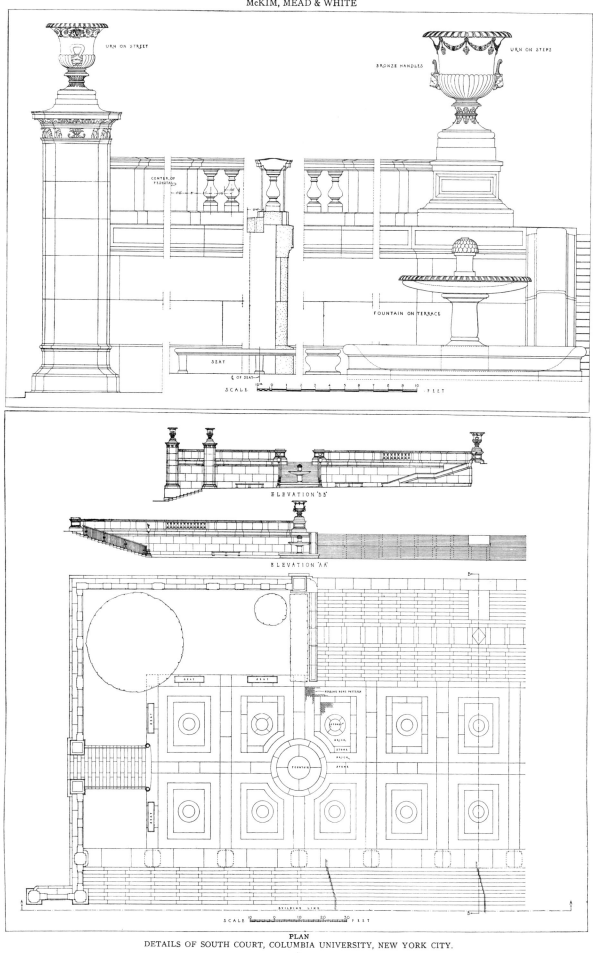

PLAN
DETAILS OF SOUTH COURT, COLUMBIA UNIVERSITY, NEW YORK CITY.

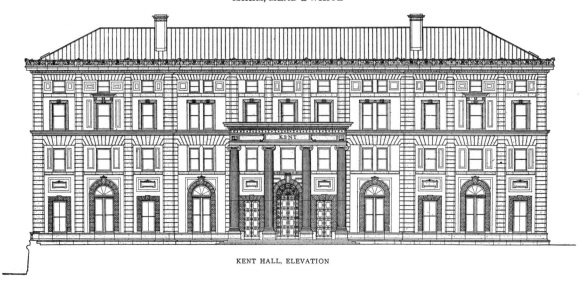

KENT HALL, ELEVATION

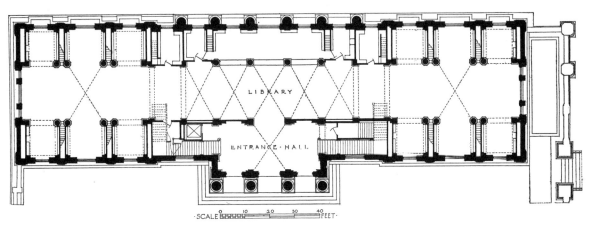

·SCALE· 0 10 20 30 40 FEET·

KENT HALL, PLAN OF FIRST FLOOR
1910

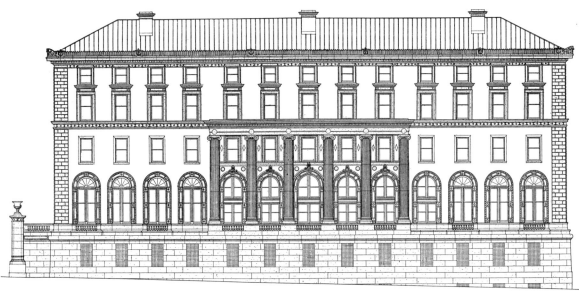

SCHOOL OF JOURNALISM, ELEVATION 1913

COLUMBIA UNIVERSITY, NEW YORK CITY.

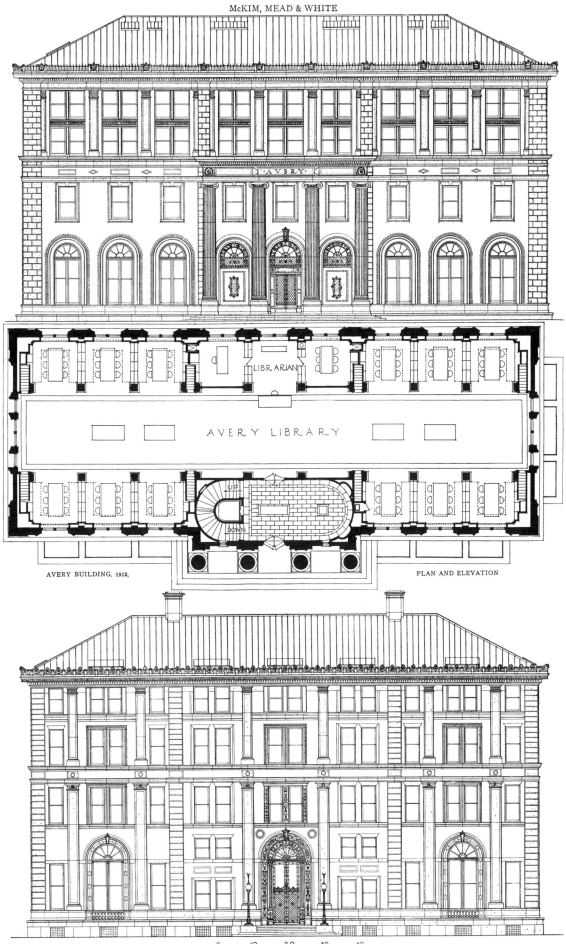

McKIM, MEAD & WHITE

·AVERY·

LIBRARIAN

AVERY LIBRARY

AVERY BUILDING, 1912,   PLAN AND ELEVATION

SCALE |⊢⊢⊢⊢⊢⊢⊢⊢| 0   10   20   30   40 |⊢⊢⊢⊢⊢⊢| FEET
PHILOSOPHY BUILDING, ELEVATION, 1910
COLUMBIA UNIVERSITY, NEW YORK CITY.

9

McKIM, MEAD & WHITE

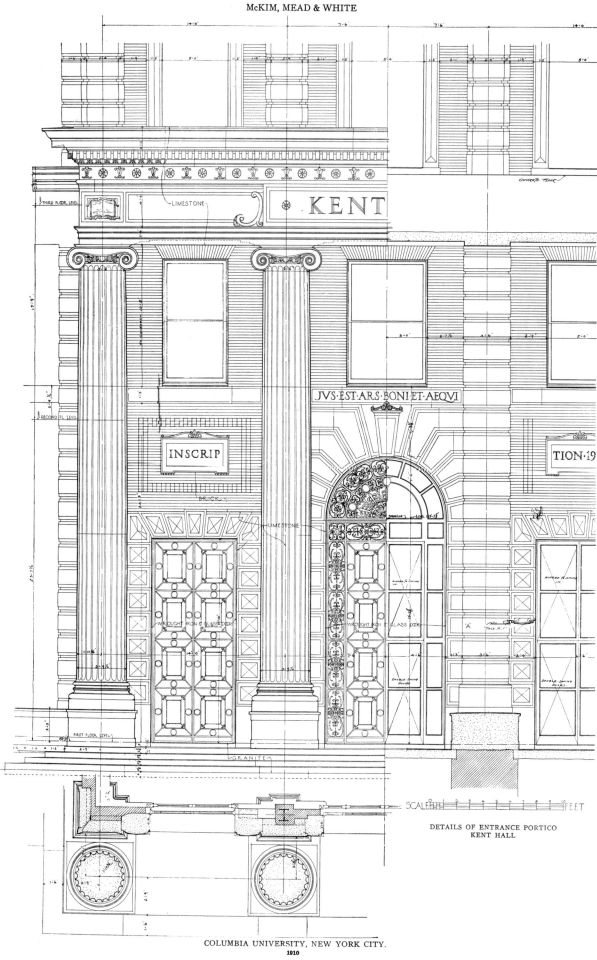

DETAILS OF ENTRANCE PORTICO
KENT HALL

COLUMBIA UNIVERSITY, NEW YORK CITY.
1910

10

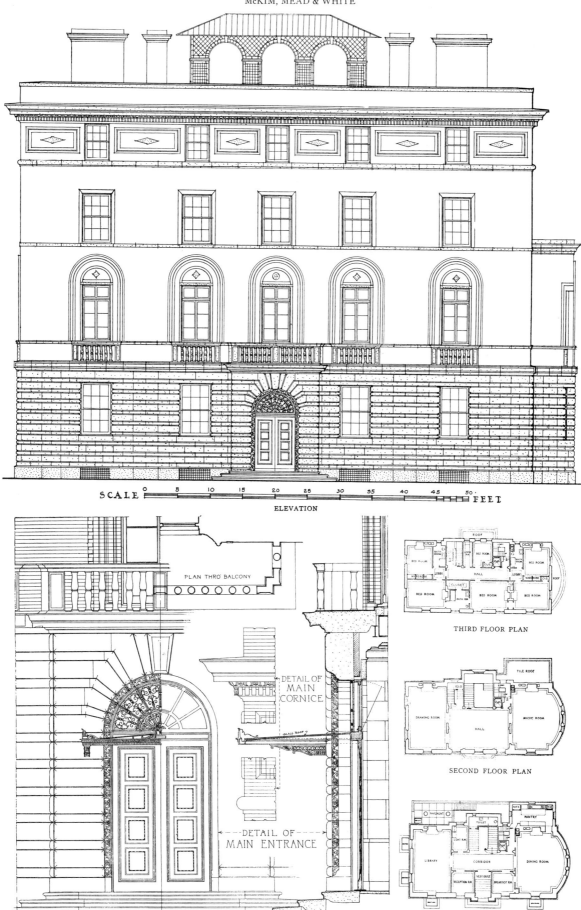

SCALE |0| 5 |10| 15 |20| 25 |30| 35 |40| 45 |50| FEET

ELEVATION

PLAN THRO' BALCONY

DETAIL OF
MAIN
CORNICE

GLASS ROOF

DETAIL OF
MAIN ENTRANCE

SCALE 12 9 6 3 0 |1| 2| 3| 4| 5| FEET

EXTERIOR DETAILS

THIRD FLOOR PLAN

SECOND FLOOR PLAN

FIRST FLOOR PLAN

PRESIDENT'S HOUSE, COLUMBIA UNIVERSITY, NEW YORK CITY.

1912

11

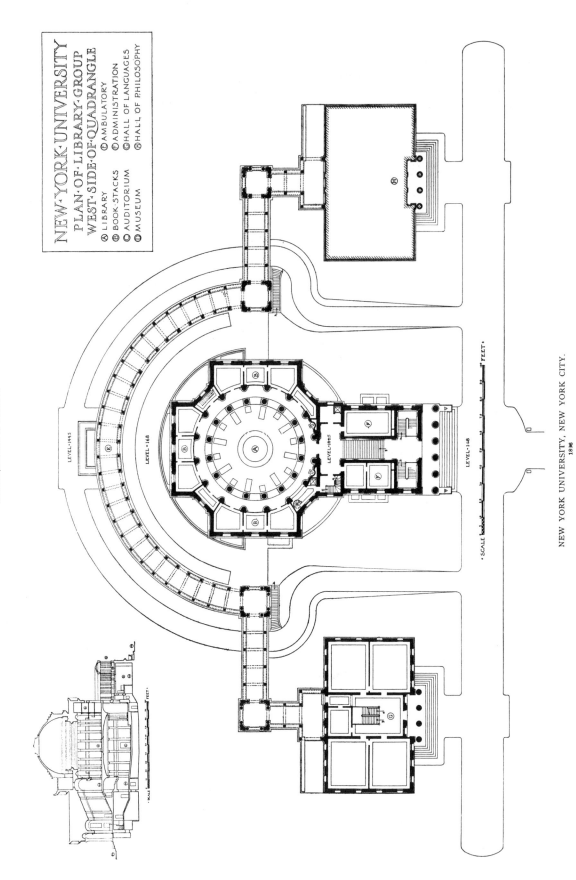

McKIM, MEAD & WHITE

NEW·YORK·UNIVERSITY
PLAN·OF·LIBRARY·GROUP
WEST·SIDE·OF·QUADRANGLE
Ⓐ LIBRARY   Ⓔ AMBULATORY
Ⓑ BOOK·STACKS   Ⓕ ADMINISTRATION
Ⓒ AUDITORIUM   Ⓖ HALL OF LANGUAGES
Ⓓ MUSEUM   Ⓗ HALL OF PHILOSOPHY

· SCALE ·   · FEET ·

NEW YORK UNIVERSITY, NEW YORK CITY.
1896

12

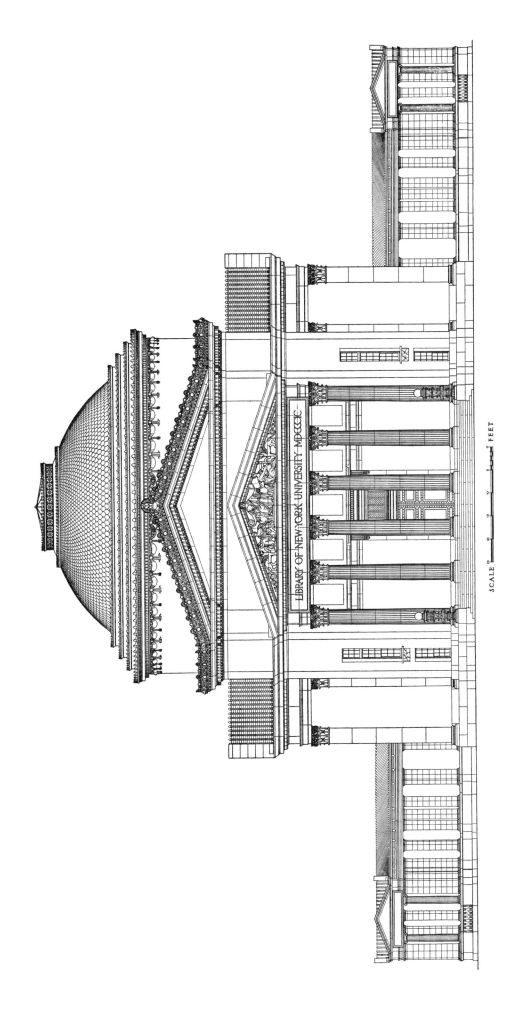

McKIM, MEAD & WHITE

LIBRARY OF NEW YORK UNIVERSITY MDCCCC

SCALE 5   10   15   20   0   FEET

NEW YORK UNIVERSITY, NEW YORK CITY.
1896

13

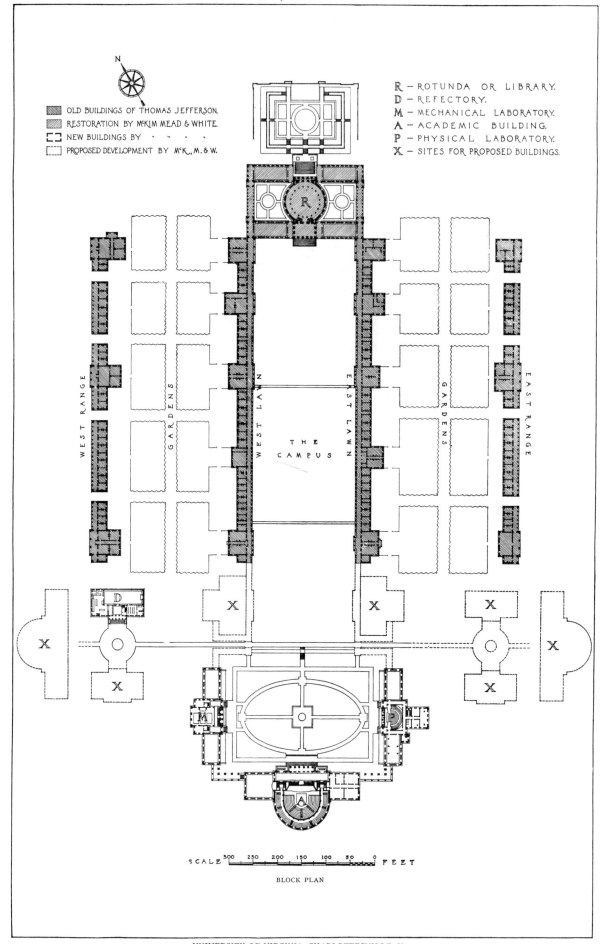

N

OLD BUILDINGS OF THOMAS JEFFERSON.
RESTORATION BY McKIM MEAD & WHITE.
NEW BUILDINGS BY " " " "
PROPOSED DEVELOPMENT BY McK., M. & W.

R — ROTUNDA OR LIBRARY.
D — REFECTORY.
M — MECHANICAL LABORATORY.
A — ACADEMIC BUILDING.
P — PHYSICAL LABORATORY.
X — SITES FOR PROPOSED BUILDINGS.

WEST RANGE

GARDENS

WEST LAWN

THE CAMPUS

EAST LAWN

GARDENS

EAST RANGE

R

D

X

X

X

X

X

X

X

X

M

A

SCALE 300 250 200 150 100 50 0 FEET

BLOCK PLAN

UNIVERSITY OF VIRGINIA. CHARLOTTESVILLE, VA.
1898

McKIM, MEAD & WHITE

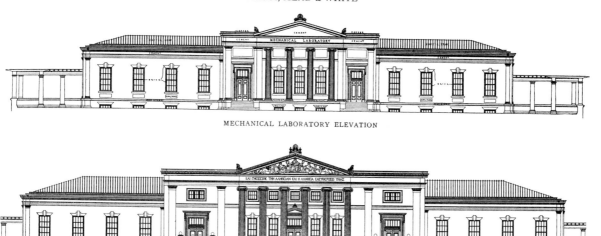

MECHANICAL LABORATORY ELEVATION

ACADEMIC BUILDING ELEVATION

MATERIALS, WALLS, RED BRICK; COLUMNS, PILASTERS, CORNICES,
DOOR AND WINDOW TRIMS, PORTLAND CEMENT STUCCO; STEPS, BLUE STONE.

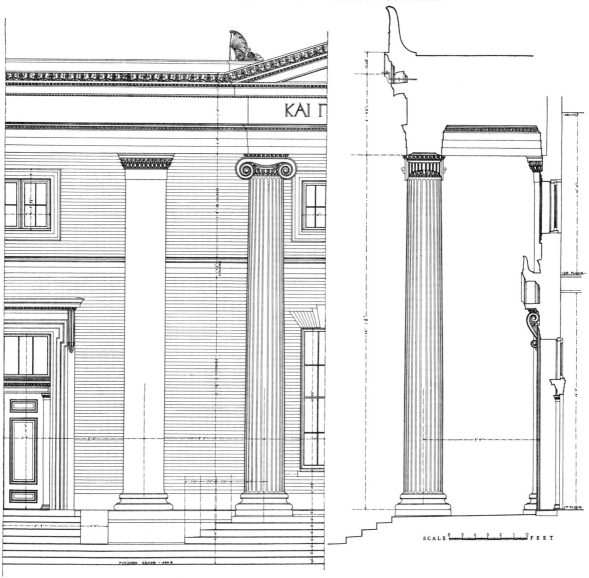

DETAIL CENTRAL PORTION, ACADEMIC BUILDING

UNIVERSITY OF VIRGINIA, CHARLOTTESVILLE, VA.

1898

15

McKIM, MEAD & WHITE

ELEVATION OF WAR COLLEGE

SCALE   FEET

· WASHINGTON · HARBOR · POTOMAC · RIVER ·

· JAMES · CREEK ·

41 ST.

P STREET

CANAL

SCALE   FEET

A : WAR COLLEGE.
B : OFFICERS QUARTERS.
C : BOILER HOUSE TEMPORARY.
D : OFFICERS MESS.
E : BACHELOR OFFICERS.
F : OFFICERS.
G : FIELD OFFICERS.
H : AGA GOA OFFICERS.

I : OBSERVATORY.
J : CHAPEL.
K : POST OFFICE & GYMNASIUM.
L : BARRACKS.
M : ENGINEER STORE-HOUSE.
N : QUARTER MASTERS & COMMIS-
        SARY STORES & OFFICES.
O : MESS HALLS.

P : HOSPITAL.
Q : ENGINEER OIL-HOUSE.
R : ENGINEER TIMBER SHED.
S : QUARTER MASTERS COAL
        & WOOD SHED.
T : ENGINEER LIFE SCHOOL.
U : ENGINEER SCHOOL.
V : ENGINEER SCHOOL POWER-HOUSE.

W : ADMINISTRATION.
X : POST BAKERY.
Y : QUARTER MASTERS SHOPS-
        INCLUDING CARPENTERS-
            PAINTERS-
            PLUMBERS-&
            BLACKSMITHS
Z : STABLE GUARD-HOUSE.

AA : QUARTER MASTERS WAGON SHED.
BB : BAND-QUARTERS.
CC : ENGINEER STABLES.
DD : QUARTER MASTERS STABLES-4.
            ENGINEERS STABLES
HH : QUARTER MASTERS OIL-HOUSE.
II : MAGAZINE. GG : POTOMA SHEDS.
FF : FLEDGED.   ERECTED.

BLOCK PLAN

ARMY WAR COLLEGE AND ENGINEERS' POST, WASHINGTON, D. C.
1908

16

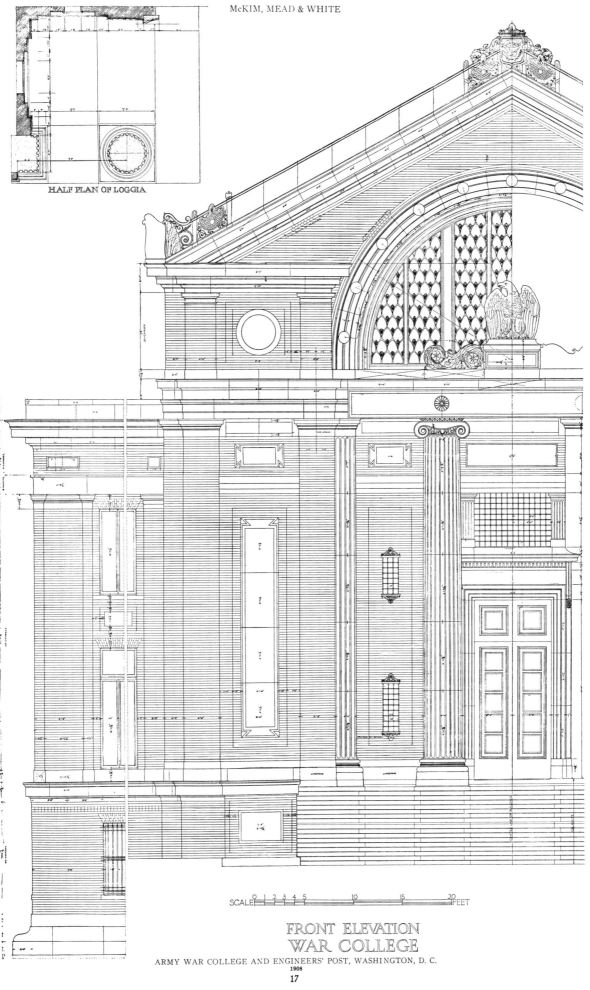

McKIM, MEAD & WHITE

HALF PLAN OF LOGGIA

SCALE 0 1 2 3 4 5 10   15   20 FEET

FRONT ELEVATION
WAR COLLEGE
ARMY WAR COLLEGE AND ENGINEERS' POST, WASHINGTON, D. C.
1908
17

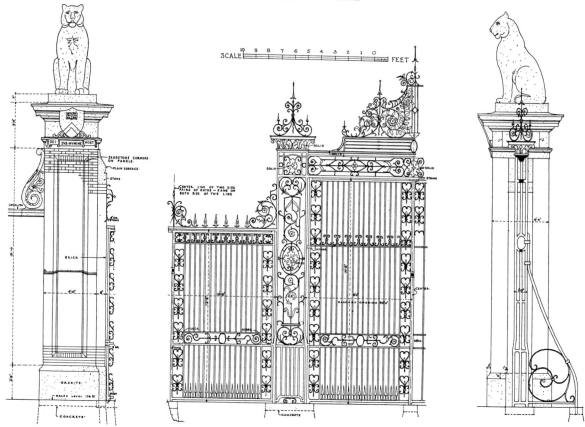

ATHLETIC FIELD GATES, PROSPECT STREET.
1913

MAIN ENTRANCE GATEWAY, NASSAU STREET.
1905
MEMORIAL GATEWAYS, PRINCETON UNIVERSITY.

18

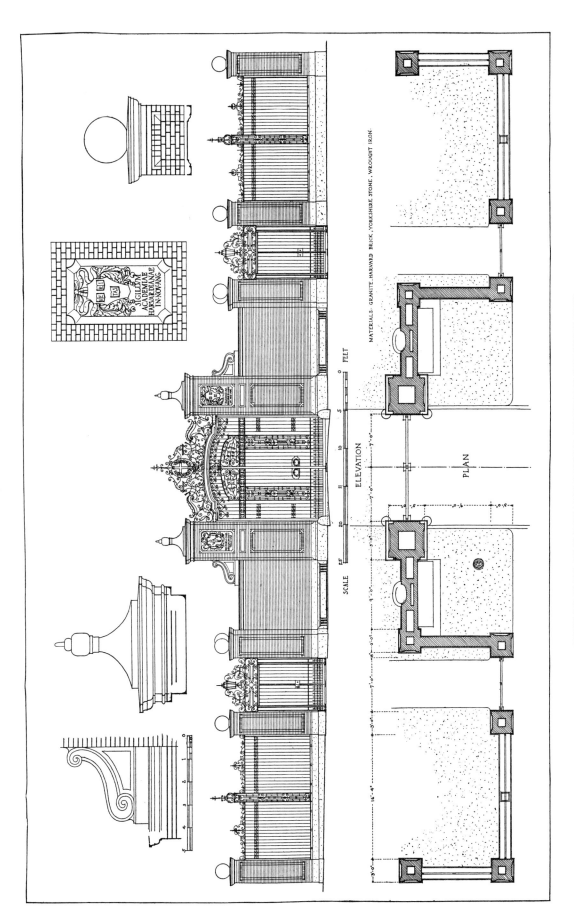

McKIM, MEAD & WHITE

MATERIALS: GRANITE, HARVARD BRICK, YORKSHIRE STONE, WROUGHT IRON.

ELEVATION

PLAN

SCALE

FEET

JOHNSTON GATES, MAIN ENTRANCE HARVARD UNIVERSITY, CAMBRIDGE, MASS.
1894

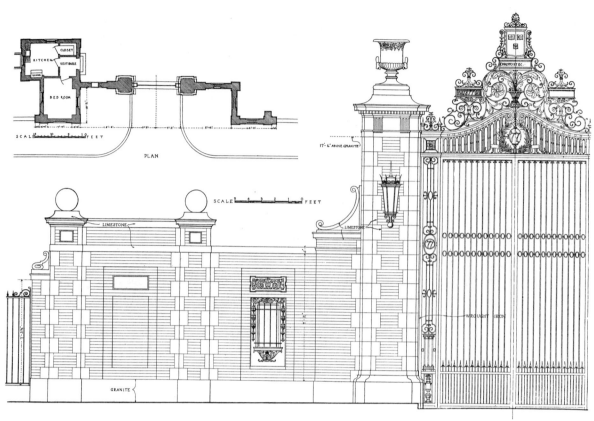

FRONT ELEVATION
CLASS OF 1877

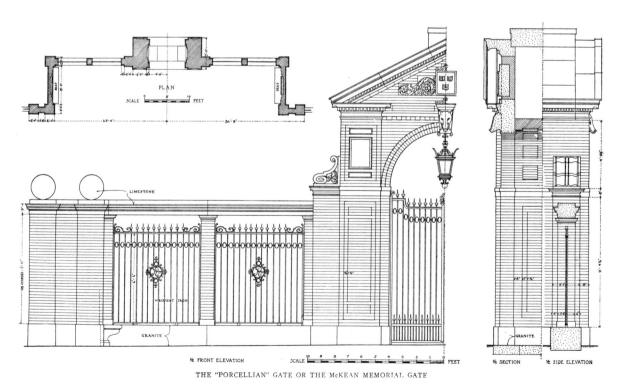

THE "PORCELLIAN" GATE OR THE McKEAN MEMORIAL GATE

MEMORIAL GATEWAYS, HARVARD UNIVERSITY, CAMBRIDGE, MASS.
1900-1901

McKIM, MEAD & WHITE

ARCHITECTVRE

ELEVATION

SCALE

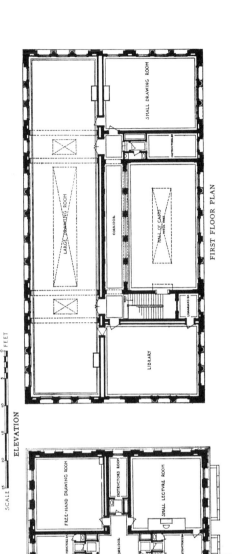

FIRST FLOOR PLAN

SMALL DRAWING ROOM

LARGE DRAWING ROOM

CORRIDOR

HALL OF CASTS

LIBRARY

SECOND FLOOR PLAN

FREE-HAND DRAWING ROOM

INSTRUCTORS ROOM

SMALL LECTVRE ROOM

CORRIDOR

LARGE LECTVRE ROOM

HALL OF CASTS

CORRIDOR

MODELLING ROOM

VESTIBULE

SAMPLE AND MODEL ROOM

ROBINSON HALL, HARVARD UNIVERSITY, CAMBRIDGE, MASS.
1904

21

SCALE |2 3 9 8 1 2 3 4 5 FEET

BRONZE ENTRANCE DOORWAY

SCALE 12 11 10 9 8 7 6 5 4 3 2 1 INCHES

ROBINSON HALL SCHOOL OF ARCHITECTURE.
HARVARD UNIVERSITY, CAMBRIDGE, MASS.
1904

McKIM, MEAD & WHITE

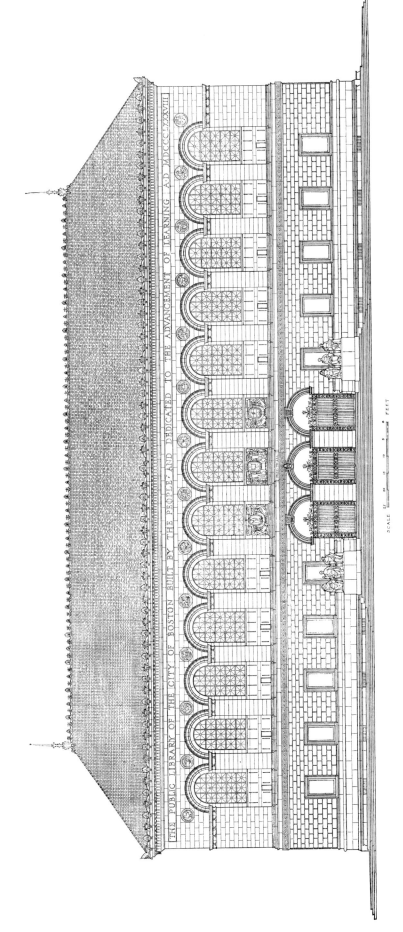

THE BOSTON PUBLIC LIBRARY, BOSTON, MASS.
DARTMOUTH STREET ELEVATION
1898

23

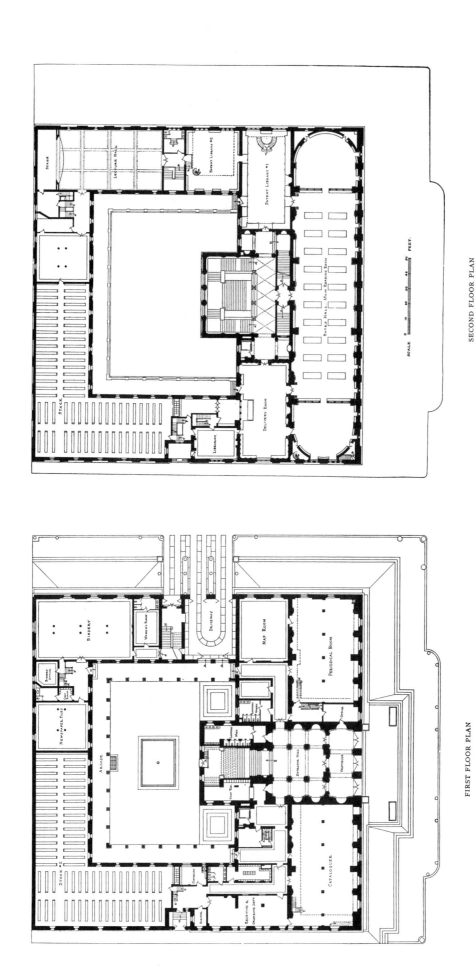

McKIM, MEAD & WHITE

SECOND FLOOR PLAN

FIRST FLOOR PLAN

THE BOSTON PUBLIC LIBRARY, BOSTON, MASS.
1898

24

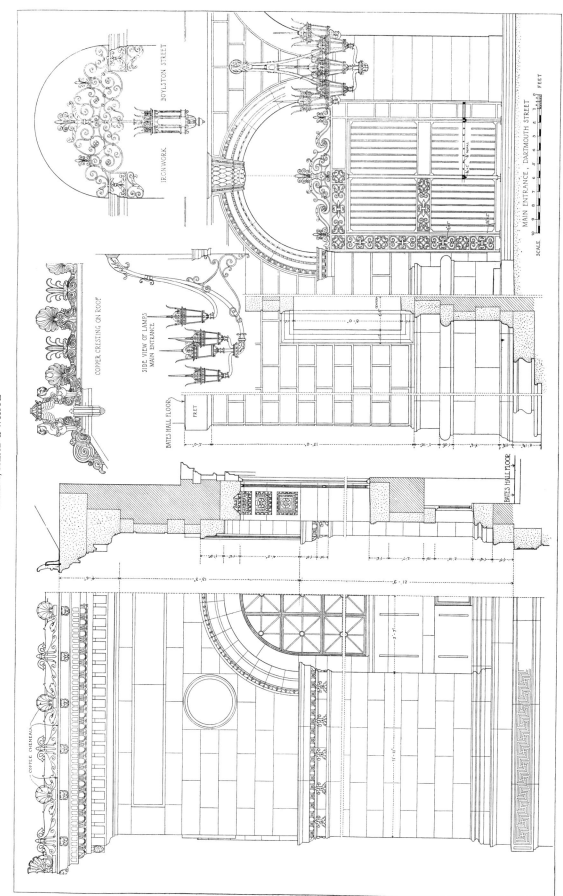

McKIM, MEAD & WHITE

EXTERIOR DETAILS

BOSTON PUBLIC LIBRARY, BOSTON, MASS.
1898

25

McKIM, MEAD & WHITE

HOMER

SOCRATES

PLAN OF CEILING

INTERIOR DETAILS, BATES HALL MAIN READING ROOM
BOSTON PUBLIC LIBRARY   BOSTON, MASS.
1898

26

McKIM, MEAD & WHITE

LOGGIA AND ROOF DETAILS

ELEVATION

SECTION

NEW YORK PUBLIC LIBRARY

NEW YO

NEW

ENTRANCE DOOR

THIRD STORY WINDOW HEAD

SECTION
ENTRANCE
DOOR

CENTER LINE OF WINDOW

BALUSTRADE
FIRST STORY WINDOW

"SCALE."

SCALE

FEET

NEW YORK PUBLIC LIBRARY, ST. GABRIEL'S BRANCH.
1906

27

McKIM, MEAD & WHITE

NEW YORK PUB

NEW YORK

SECTION

MT. MORRIS BRANCH

ELEVATION

FEET

SCALE

SECTION

NEW·YORK·PUBLIC·LIBRARY·

HAMILTON GRANGE BRANCH

ELEVATION

SCALE

FEET

NEW YORK PUBLIC LIBRARY, BRANCH BUILDINGS.

28

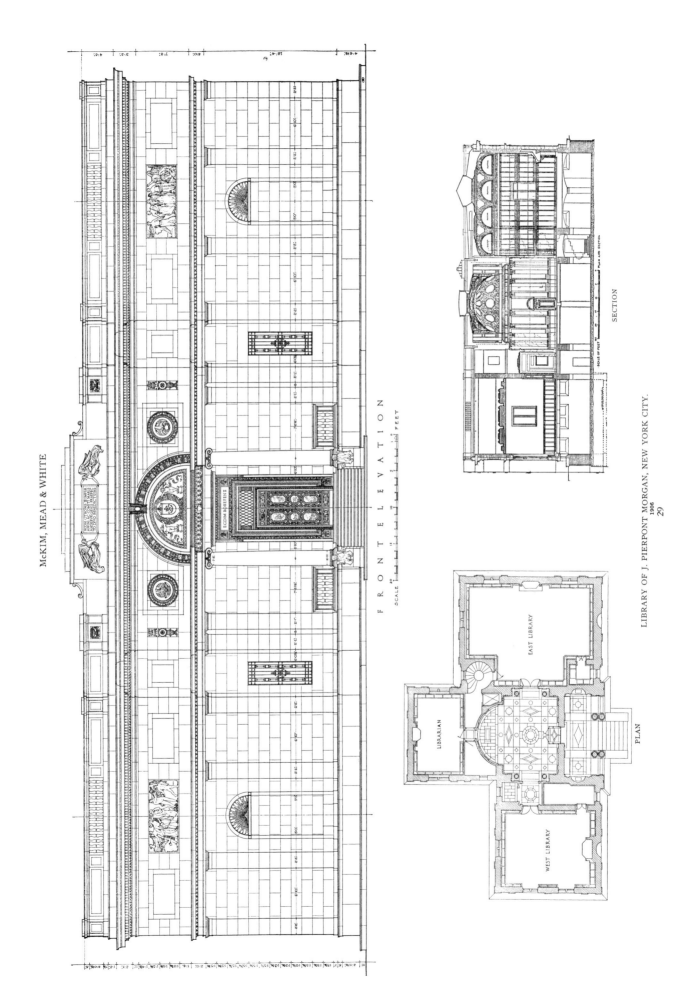

McKIM, MEAD & WHITE

FRONT ELEVATION

SECTION

PLAN

LIBRARY OF J. PIERPONT MORGAN, NEW YORK CITY.
1906
29

EAST LIBRARY

LIBRARIAN

WEST LIBRARY

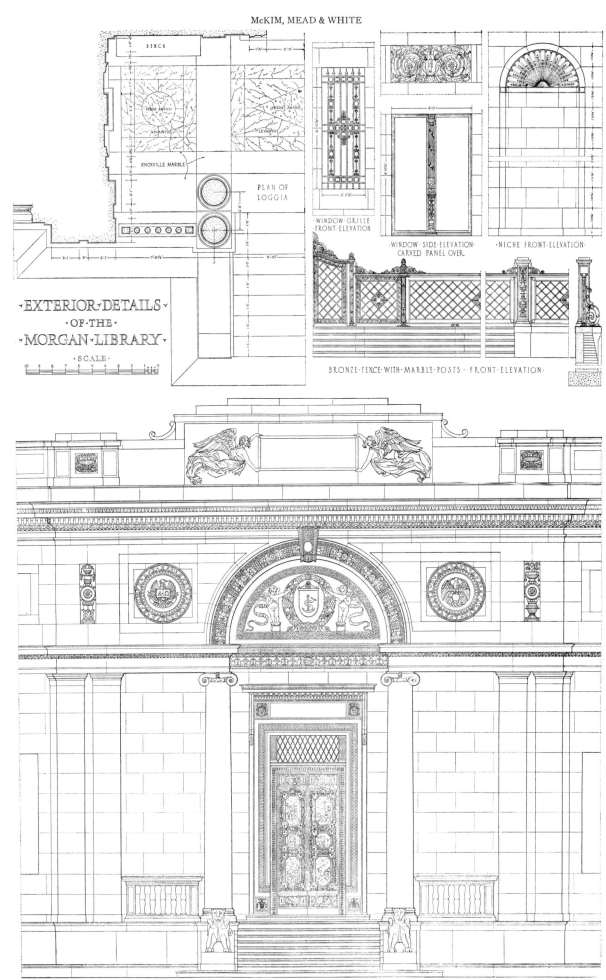

McKIM, MEAD & WHITE

BENCH

VERDE ANTICO

LEVANTO

KNOXVILLE MARBLE

(VERDE ANTICO)

LEVANTO

PLAN OF
LOGGIA

EXTERIOR·DETAILS
·OF·THE·
·MORGAN·LIBRARY·
·SCALE·

WINDOW·GRILLE
FRONT·ELEVATION

WINDOW·SIDE·ELEVATION·
CARVED·PANEL·OVER·

NICHE·FRONT·ELEVATION·

BRONZE·FENCE·WITH·MARBLE·POSTS·FRONT·ELEVATION·

LIBRARY OF J. PIERPONT MORGAN, NEW YORK CITY.
1906
30

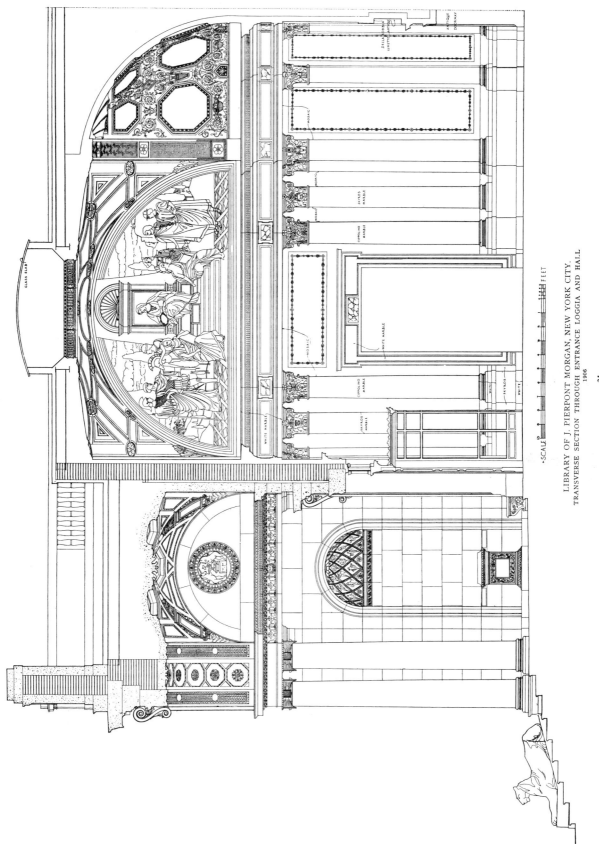

McKIM, MEAD & WHITE

GLASS SLAB

LIBRARY OF J. PIERPONT MORGAN, NEW YORK CITY.
TRANSVERSE SECTION THROUGH ENTRANCE LOGGIA AND HALL
1906

SCALE FEET

31

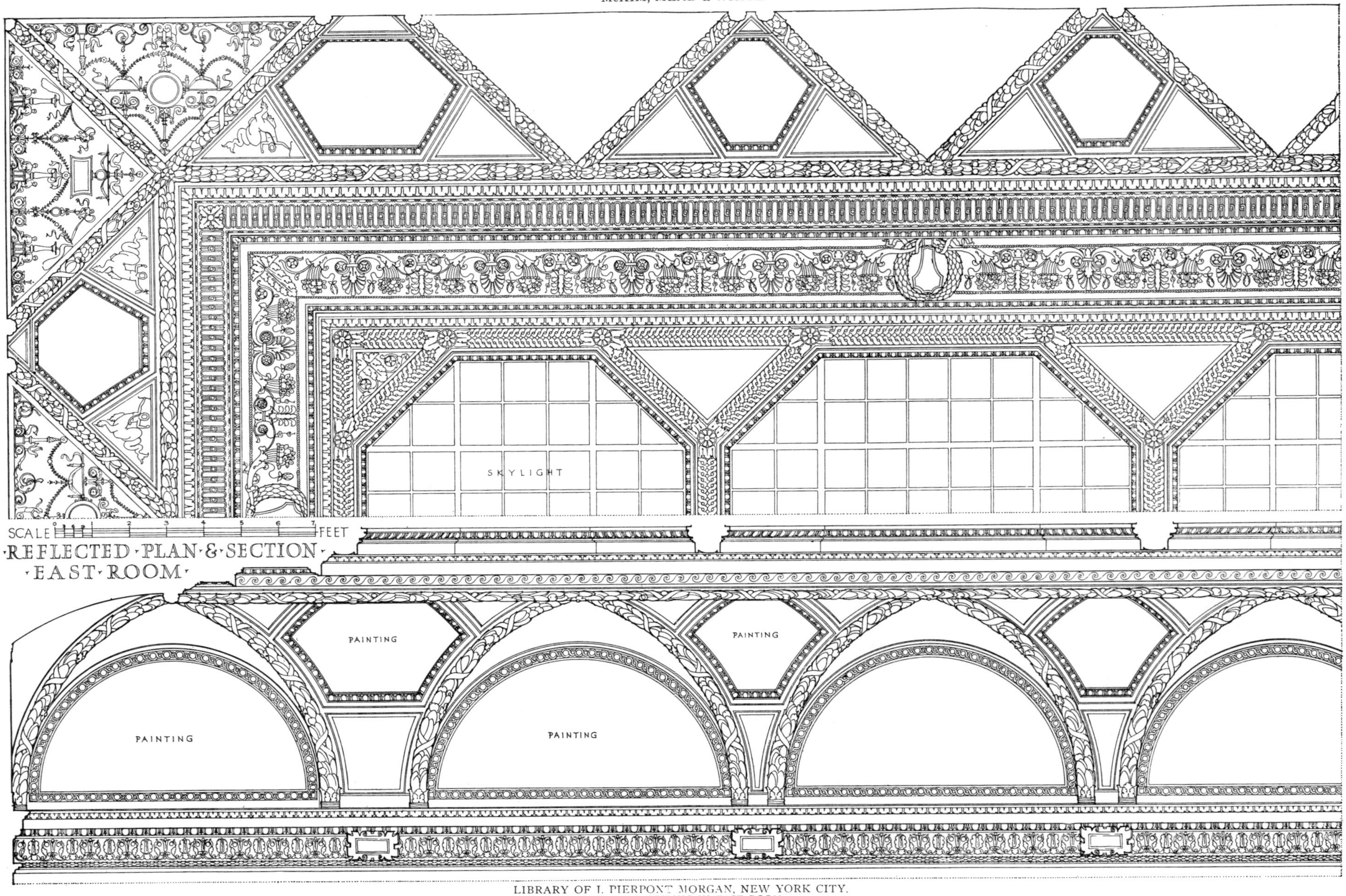

McKIM, MEAD & WHITE

SKYLIGHT

PAINTING

PAINTING

PAINTING

PAINTING

PAINTING

SCALE

FEET

·REFLECTED·PLAN·&·SECTION·
·EAST·ROOM·

LIBRARY OF J. PIERPONT MORGAN, NEW YORK CITY.
DETAIL OF CEILING IN EAST ROOM
1906

32

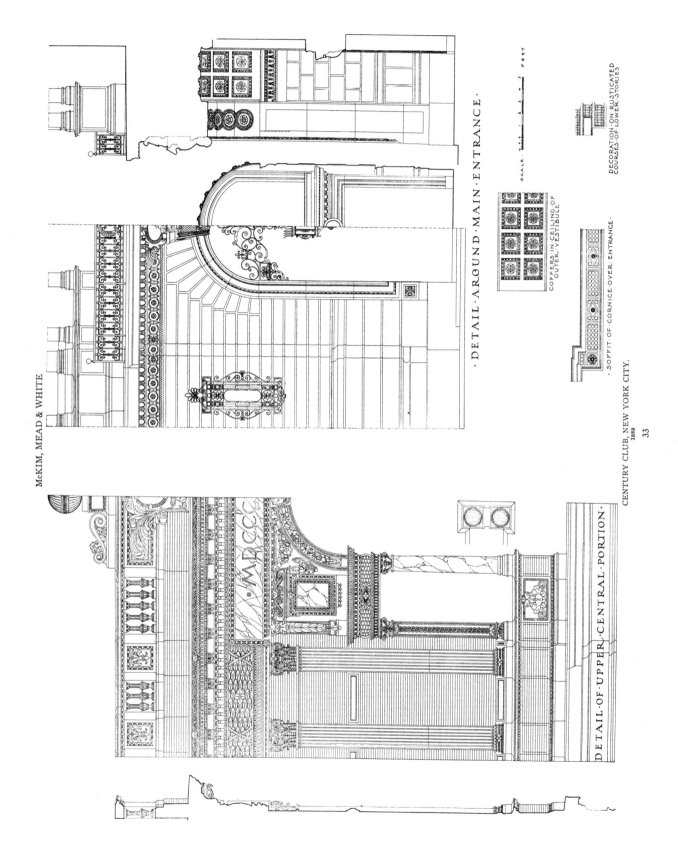

McKIM, MEAD & WHITE

· DETAIL · AROUND · MAIN · ENTRANCE ·

DECORATION · ON · RUSTICATED
COURSES · OF · LOWER · STORIES

SCALE   FEET

COFFERS · IN · CEILING · OF
OUTER · VESTIBULE

· SOFFIT · OF · CORNICE · OVER · ENTRANCE ·

CENTURY CLUB, NEW YORK CITY.
1889

· DETAIL · OF · UPPER · CENTRAL · PORTION ·

MDCCC

33

McKIM, MEAD & WHITE

·MDCCCLXXXIX·

CENTURY CLUB, NEW YORK CITY.
1889
34

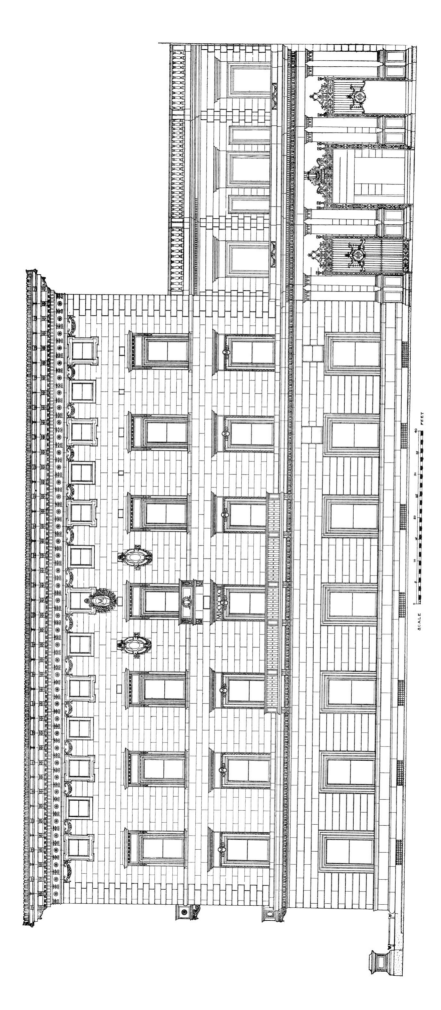

McKIM, MEAD & WHITE

SIXTIETH STREET ELEVATION
METROPOLITAN CLUB, NEW YORK CITY.
1894

SCALE

35

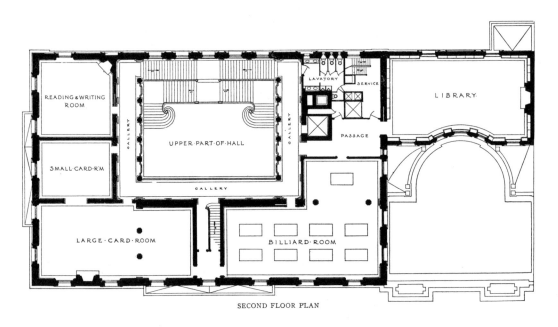

SECOND FLOOR PLAN

METROPOLITAN CLUB, NEW YORK CITY.

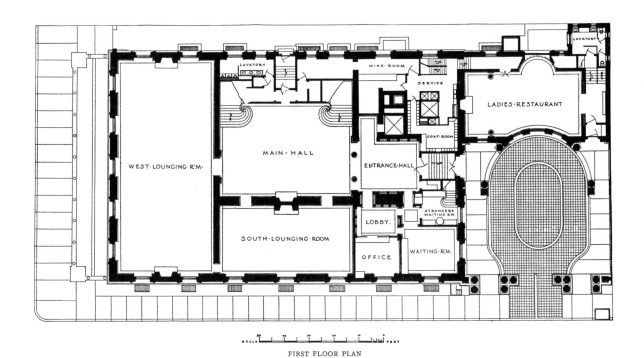

FIRST FLOOR PLAN

METROPOLITAN CLUB, NEW YORK CITY.
1894

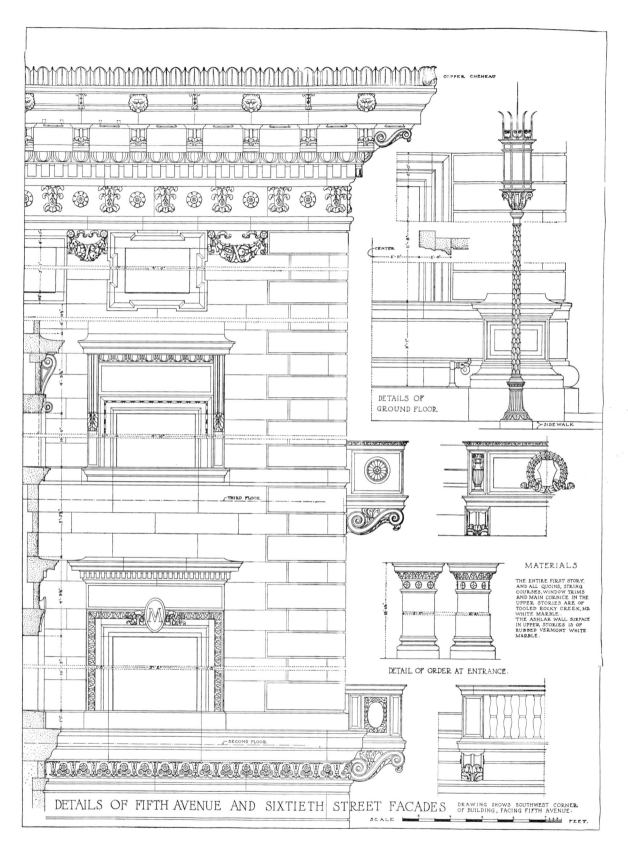

COPPER CHENEAU

DETAILS OF
GROUND FLOOR

CENTER

MATERIALS

THE ENTIRE FIRST STORY,
AND ALL QUOINS, STRING
COURSES, WINDOW TRIMS
AND MAIN CORNICE IN THE
UPPER STORIES ARE OF
TOOLED ROCKY CREEK, MD.
WHITE MARBLE.
THE ASHLAR WALL SURFACE
IN UPPER STORIES IS OF
RUBBED VERMONT WHITE
MARBLE.

DETAIL OF ORDER AT ENTRANCE.

THIRD FLOOR

SECOND FLOOR

DETAILS OF FIFTH AVENUE AND SIXTIETH STREET FACADES

DRAWING SHOWS SOUTHWEST CORNER
OF BUILDING, FACING FIFTH AVENUE.

SCALE   FEET.

METROPOLITAN CLUB, NEW YORK CITY.
1894

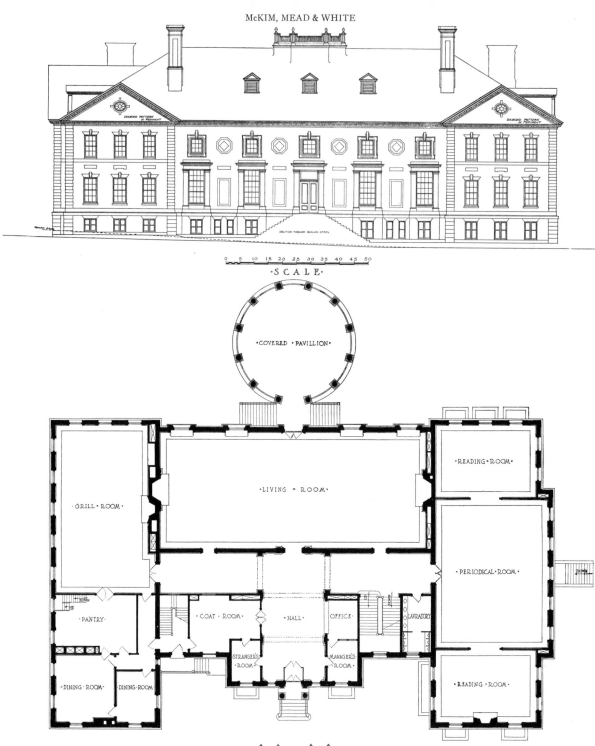

·SCALE·

·COVERED·PAVILLION·

GRILL·ROOM·

·LIVING·ROOM·

·READING·ROOM·

·PERIODICAL·ROOM·

·PANTRY·

·COAT·ROOM·   ·HALL·   OFFICE   LAVRATORY

STRANGER'S ROOM   MANAGER'S ROOM

·DINING·ROOM·   DINING·ROOM·

·READING·ROOM·

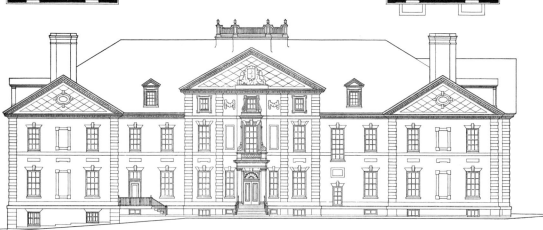

THE HARVARD UNION, CAMBRIDGE, MASS.
1902

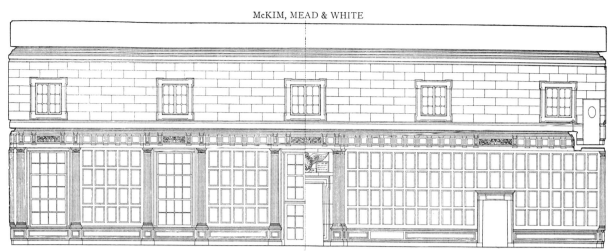

McKIM, MEAD & WHITE

·½ SOUTH WALL·   ·½ NORTH WALL·

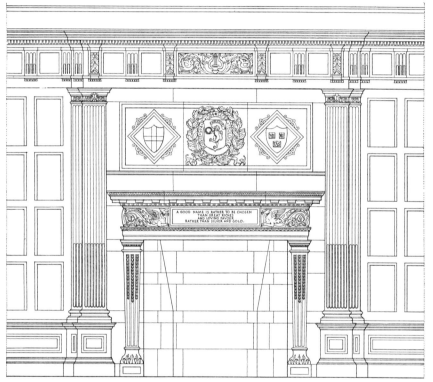

A GOOD NAME IS RATHER TO BE CHOSEN
THAN GREAT RICHES
AND LOVING FAVOUR
RATHER THAN SILVER AND GOLD.

·ELEVATION OF MANTEL ON WEST WALL·

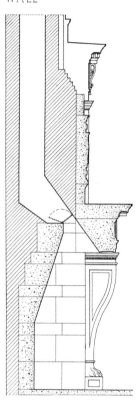

·SECTION·

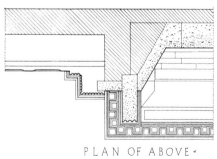

·PLAN OF ABOVE·

SCALE ▭▭▭▭▭▭▭▭▭ FOR DETAILS

SCALE ▭▭▭▭▭▭ FOR WALLS

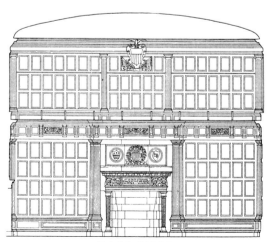

·EAST WALL·

DETAILS OF LIVING ROOM
THE HARVARD UNION, CAMBRIDGE, MASS.
NOTE: FOR "DINING HALL" READ "LIVING ROOM" ON PAGE NO. 160
1902

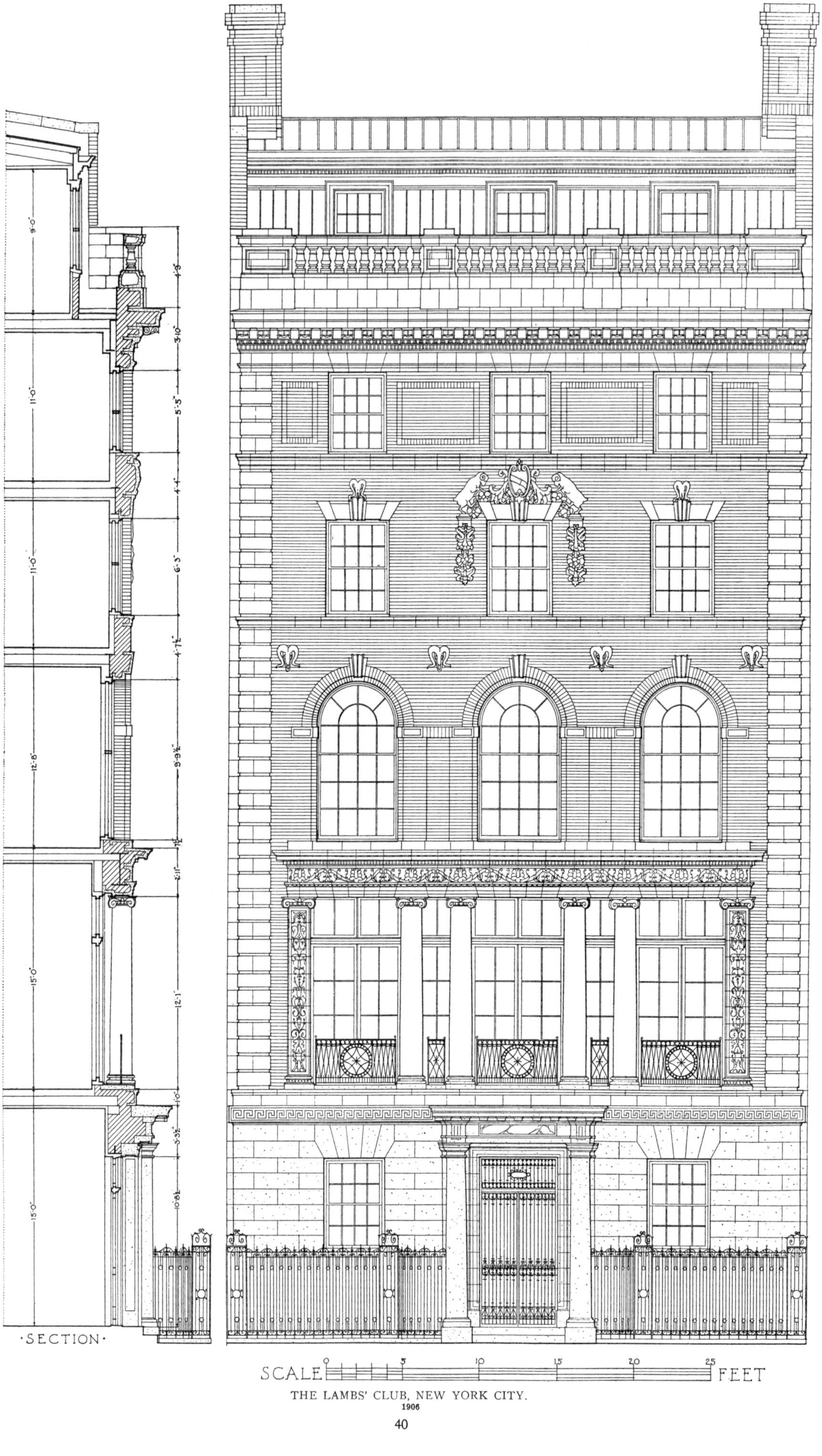

·SECTION·

SCALE |————|————|————|————|————| FEET

THE LAMBS' CLUB, NEW YORK CITY.

1906

SCALE 25 20 15 10 5 0 FEET

·PLANS·OF·GROVND·AND·THIRD·FLOOR·FRONTS·

THE HARMONIE CLUB, NEW YORK CITY.
FRONT ELEVATION
1906

McKIM, MEAD & WHITE

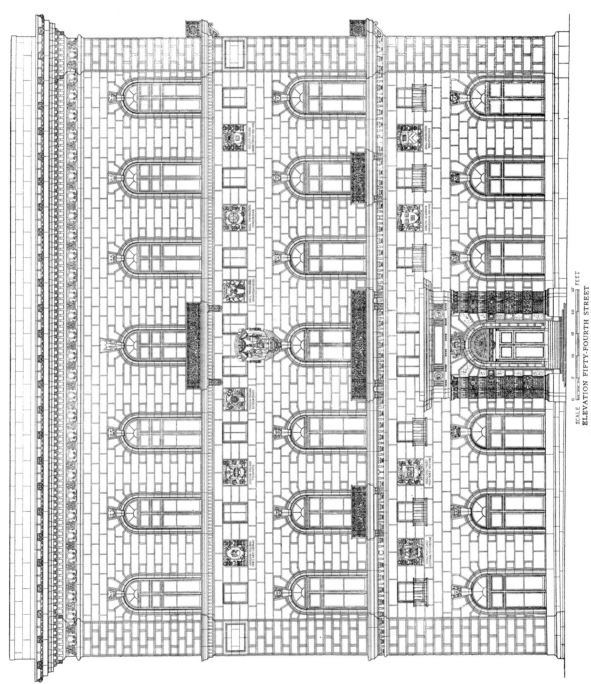

SCALE
0   5   10   15   20   25 FEET
ELEVATION FIFTY-FOURTH STREET
UNIVERSITY CLUB, NEW YORK CITY.
1900

42

McKIM, MEAD & WHITE

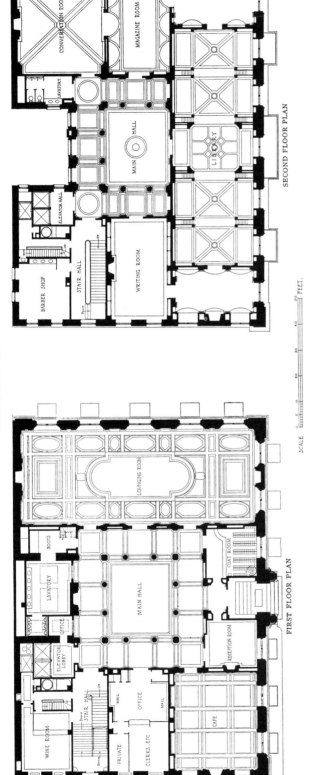

FIRST FLOOR PLAN

SECOND FLOOR PLAN

SCALE [_____] FEET.

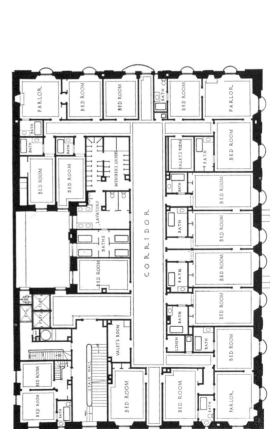

THIRD FLOOR PLAN

FIRST BEDROOM FLOOR PLAN

UNIVERSITY CLUB, NEW YORK CITY.
1900

43

CHRISTO
VE RI TAS
ET ECCLESIÆ

TERRAS
IRRADIENT

SECTION THRO' ENTRANCE

·PLAN·

SCALE FEET

·SECTION· ·FIFTH AVE ELEVATION· ·MAIN ENTRANCE·

DETAILS OF EXTERIOR STONEWORK
UNIVERSITY CLUB, NEW YORK CITY.
1900

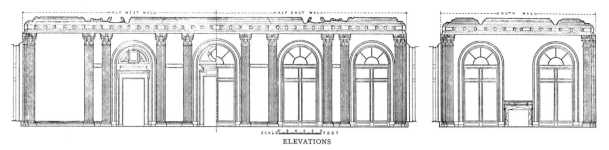

ELEVATIONS

UPPER CORNICE AND CEILING PLASTER
WITH INSERTS OF MARBLE.

HALF ELEVATION
OF WINDOW

HALF ELEVATION
OF DOOR WAY
TO HALL

WOOD WORK
OF ITALIAN WALNUT
CARVED AND GILDED

WALLS
RED VELVET

DOOR WAY ON AXIS
OF MAIN HALL

MARBLE DOOR TRIMS
AND MANTELS
BROWN NUMIDIAN

SECTION THRO.
WINDOW.

PLAN AT WINDOW   PLAN AT DOOR   PLAN AT DOOR

SCALE 10 9 8 7 6 5 4 3 2 1 0 FEET

DETAIL OF WALL AND ONE FOURTH OF CEILING

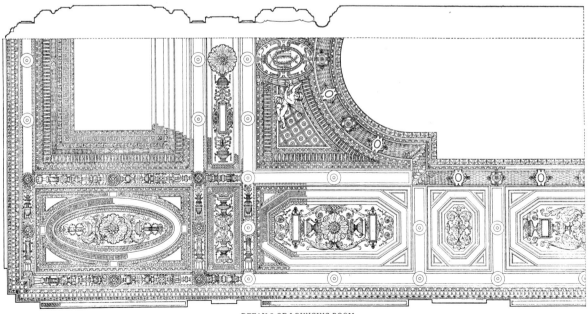

DETAILS OF LOUNGING ROOM

THE UNIVERSITY CLUB, NEW YORK CITY.
1900

45

HALF ELEVATION OF NORTH WALL, AND DETAIL OF PORTION OF CEILING, MAIN DINING ROOM

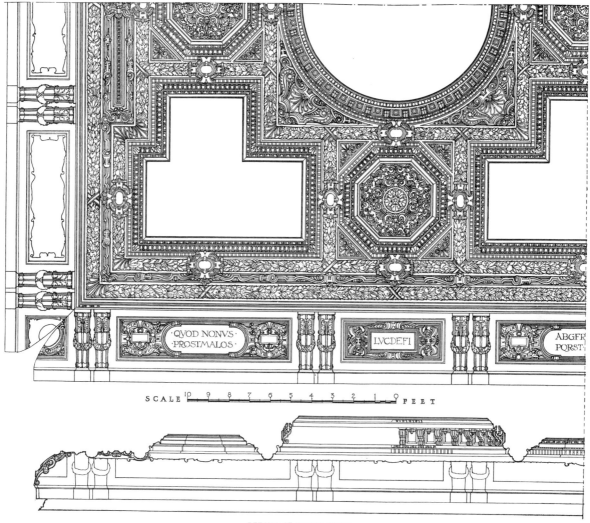

SCALE 10 9 8 7 6 5 4 3 2 1 0 FEET

DETAILS OF DINING ROOM

THE UNIVERSITY CLUB, NEW YORK CITY.
1900

46

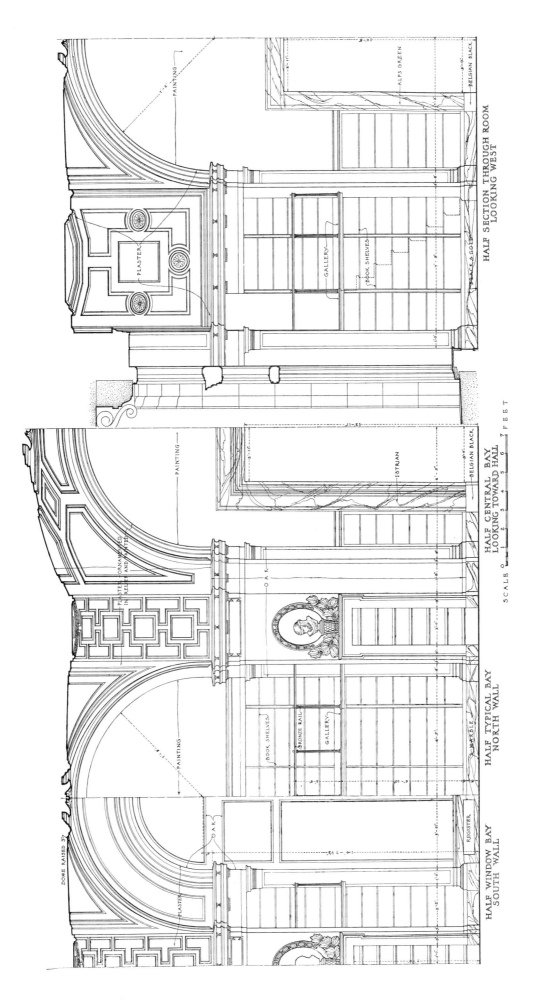

McKIM, MEAD & WHITE

PAINTING

PLASTER ORNAMENTED IN RELIEF AND PAINTED

PAINTING

DOME RAISED 3½

PLASTER

OAK

BOOK SHELVES

BRONZE RAIL

GALLERY

MARBLE

ISTRIAN

BELGIAN BLACK

OAK

REGISTER

HALF WINDOW BAY
SOUTH WALL

HALF TYPICAL BAY
NORTH WALL

HALF CENTRAL BAY
LOOKING TOWARD HALL

SCALE 0 1 2 3 4 5 6 7 FEET

PAINTING

PLASTER

GALLERY

BOOK SHELVES

ALPS GREEN

BELGIAN BLACK

BLACK & GOLD

HALF SECTION THROUGH ROOM
LOOKING WEST

UNIVERSITY CLUB, NEW YORK CITY.
DETAILS OF THE LIBRARY
1900

47

UPPER PART OF CORNICE AND VAULTED CEILING, PLASTER.

WHITE NORWEGIAN MARBLE

BRONZE CAPITALS

TERRAZZO

SIENA MARBLE

TERRAZZO
3-COLORS

WHITE MARBLE INLAY

SHAFTS OF
COLUMNS AND
PILASTERS
CONNEMARA
MARBLE

CARVED PANEL ABOVE
WHITE STATUARY MARBLE

BRICK LINING
ISTRIAN STONE MANTEL

WHITE NORWEGIAN MARBLE

MANTEL IN 1ST STORY HALL

4 3 2 1 0
SCALE

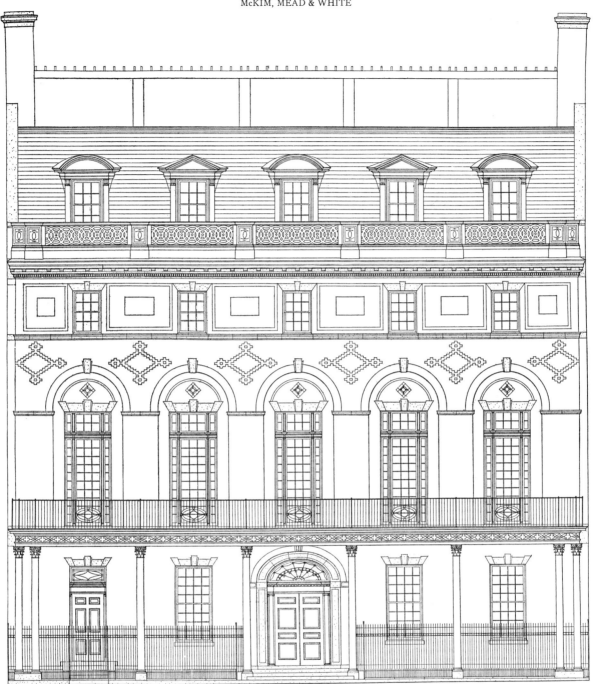

ELEVATION

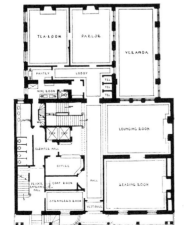

FIRST FLOOR PLAN

SECOND FLOOR PLAN

THE COLONY CLUB, NEW YORK CITY.
1906

CAST IRON

MARBLE — WOOD →

· S E C T I O N ·

SECTION · THRO
MAIN · DOORWAY

· P L A N ·

SCALE   0 1 2 3 4 5 6 7 8 9 10   FEET

EXTERIOR DETAILS
THE COLONY CLUB, NEW YORK CITY.
1906

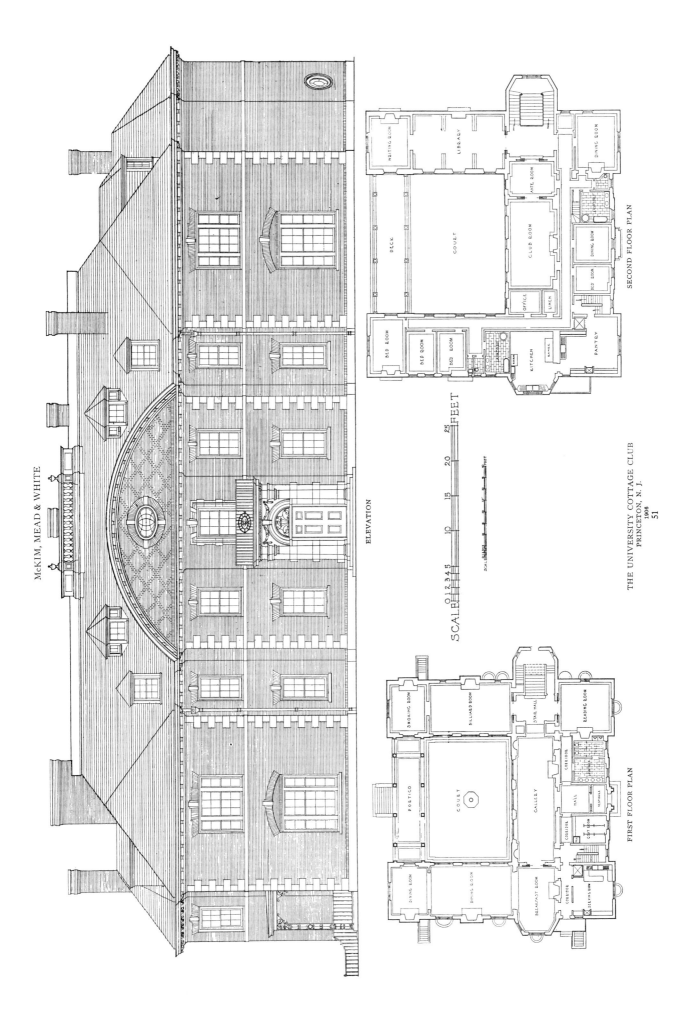

McKIM, MEAD & WHITE

ELEVATION

SCALE 0 1 2 3 4 5   10   15   20   25   FEET

SCALE   FEET

SECOND FLOOR PLAN

WRITING ROOM

LIBRARY

DECK

COURT

ANTE ROOM

CLUB ROOM

OFFICE

LINEN

KITCHEN

RANGE

LAVATORY

PANTRY

BED ROOM

DINING ROOM

BED ROOM

BED ROOM

BED ROOM

FIRST FLOOR PLAN

SMOKING ROOM

BILLIARD ROOM

STAIR HALL

READING ROOM

PORTICO

COURT

GALLERY

CORRIDOR

HALL

VESTIBULE

CORRIDOR

COAT ROOM

DINING ROOM

DINING ROOM

BREAKFAST ROOM

CORRIDOR

READING ROOM

THE UNIVERSITY COTTAGE CLUB
PRINCETON, N. J.
1906
51

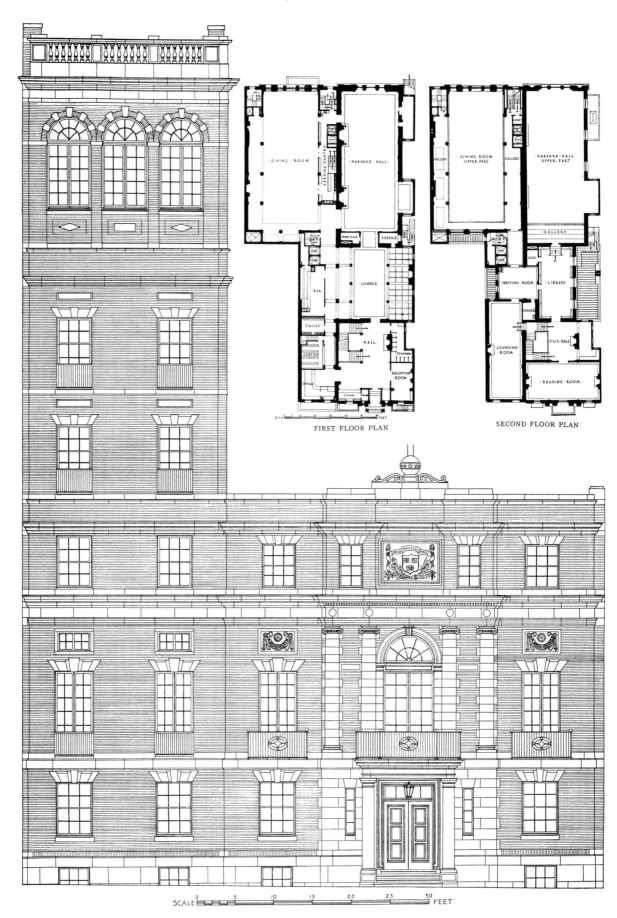

FIRST FLOOR PLAN

SECOND FLOOR PLAN

SCALE [===] 0   5   10   15   20   25   30   FEET

THE HARVARD CLUB, NEW YORK CITY.
ORIGINAL BUILDING ON RIGHT, 1902, ADDITION ON LEFT, 1915.

McKIM, MEAD & WHITE

LONGITUDINAL SECTION

·SCALE· FEET·

·SIDE·

·SCALE·
·FEET·

·PLAN·

·SECTION·

·DETAIL·OF·MANTEL·
·DETAIL·OF·NORTH·WINDOW·

HARVARD HALL, LOUNGING ROOM OF HARVARD CLUB, NEW YORK CITY.
1905

53

McKIM, MEAD & WHITE

SCALE 0 5 10 15 20 25 30 35 40 FEET.

ELEVATION

FOURTH FLOOR PLAN

THIRD FLOOR PLAN

SECOND FLOOR PLAN

FIRST FLOOR PLAN

THE RACQUET AND TENNIS CLUB, NEW YORK CITY.

1917

54

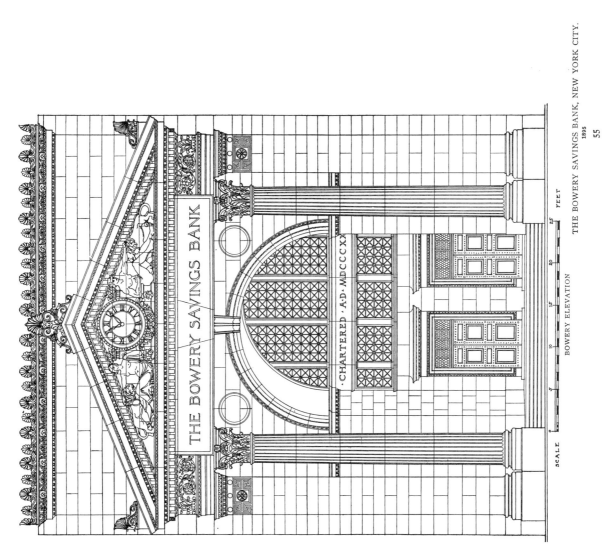

McKIM, MEAD & WHITE

THE BOWERY SAVINGS BANK, NEW YORK CITY.
1895

55

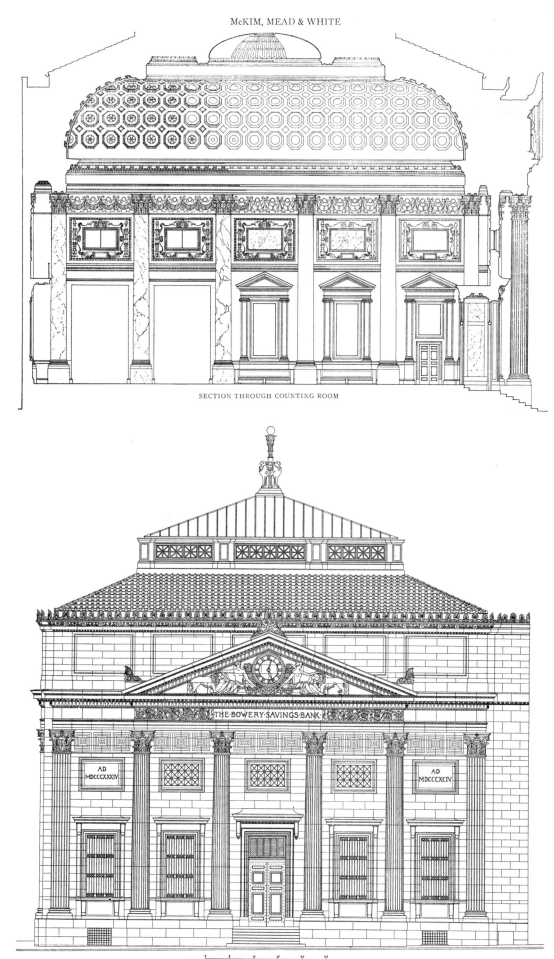

SECTION THROUGH COUNTING ROOM

THE·BOWERY·SAVINGS·BANK·

AD
MDCCCXXXIV

AD
MDCCCXCIV

SCALE   FEET.
GRAND STREET ELEVATION
THE BOWERY SAVINGS BANK, NEW YORK CITY.
1895

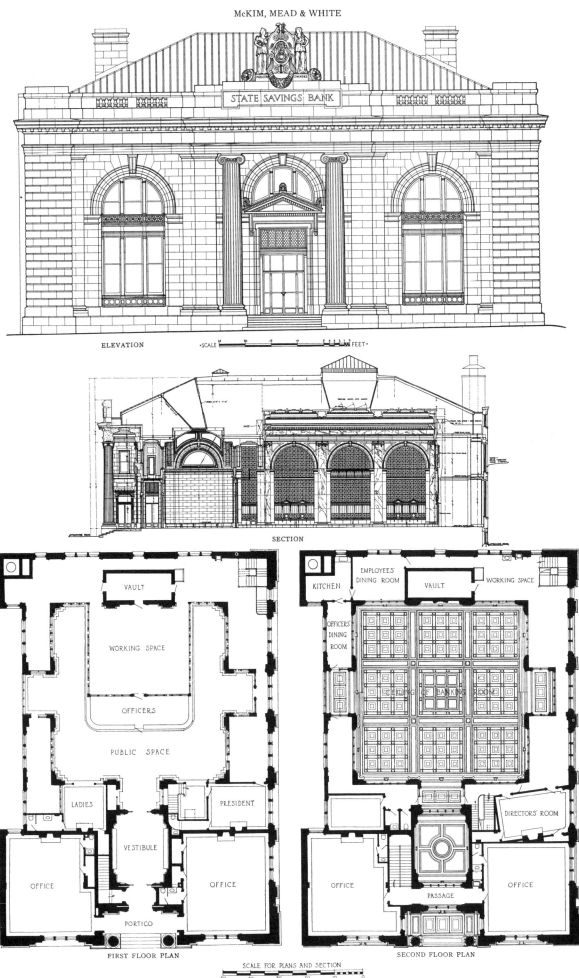

McKIM, MEAD & WHITE

STATE SAVINGS BANK

ELEVATION   ·SCALE·   ·FEET·

SECTION

FIRST FLOOR PLAN

VAULT

WORKING SPACE

OFFICERS

PUBLIC SPACE

LADIES

PRESIDENT

VESTIBULE

OFFICE

OFFICE

PORTICO

SECOND FLOOR PLAN

KITCHEN

EMPLOYEES' DINING ROOM

VAULT

WORKING SPACE

OFFICERS' DINING ROOM

CEILING OF BANKING ROOM

DIRECTORS' ROOM

OFFICE

OFFICE

PASSAGE

SCALE FOR PLANS AND SECTION

THE STATE SAVINGS BANK, DETROIT, MICHIGAN.
1900

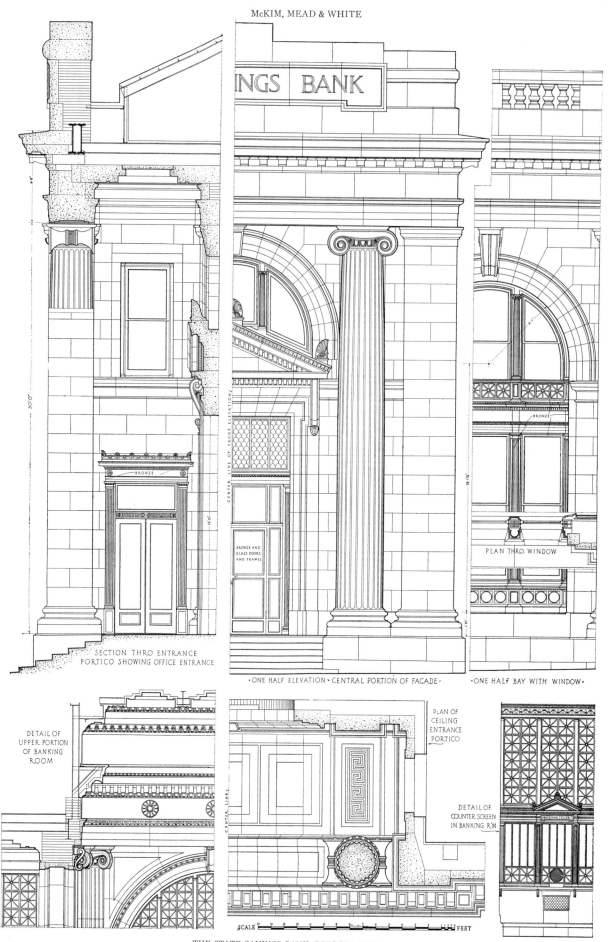

INGS | BANK

CENTER LINE OF FRONT ELEVATION

BRONZE AND
GLASS DOORS
AND FRAMES

BRONZE

SECTION THRO ENTRANCE
PORTICO SHOWING OFFICE ENTRANCE.

·ONE HALF ELEVATION· CENTRAL PORTION OF FACADE·

·ONE HALF BAY WITH WINDOW·

PLAN THRO. WINDOW

BRONZE

DETAIL OF
UPPER PORTION
OF BANKING
ROOM

PLAN OF
CEILING
ENTRANCE
PORTICO

DETAIL OF
COUNTER SCREEN
IN BANKING R'M

CENTER LINE

SCALE FEET

THE STATE SAVINGS BANK, DETROIT, MICHIGAN.
EXTERIOR AND INTERIOR DETAILS
1900

SCALE |25| |20| |15| |10| |5| | FEET

FIFTH AVENUE ELEVATION

BUILDING FOR THE KNICKERBOCKER TRUST CO., NEW YORK CITY.
1904

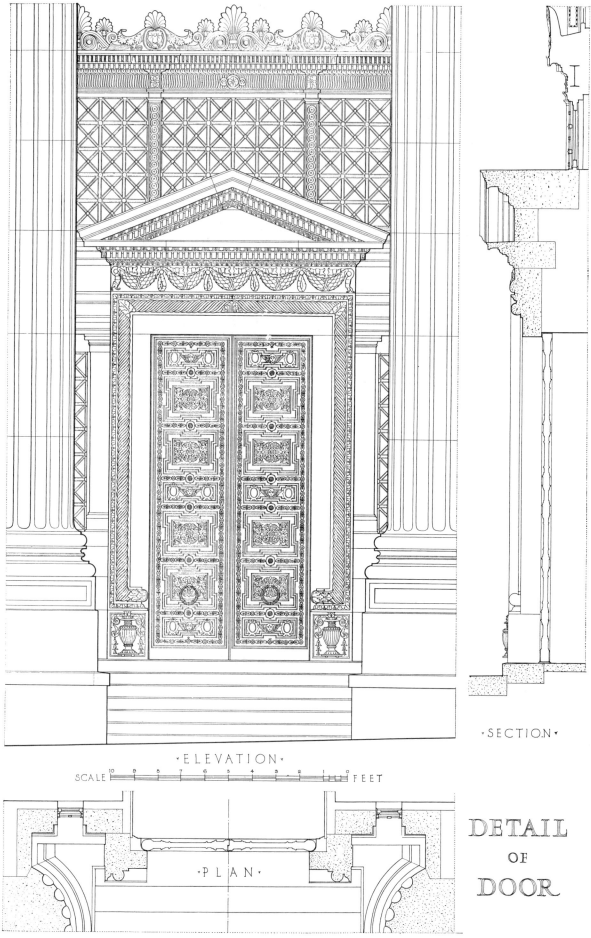

· ELEVATION ·

SCALE 10 9 8 7 6 5 4 3 2 1 0 FEET

· SECTION ·

· PLAN ·

DETAIL
OF
DOOR

BUILDING FOR THE KNICKERBOCKER TRUST CO., NEW YORK CITY.
BRONZE ENTRANCE DOORS WITH MARBLE TRIM
1904
60

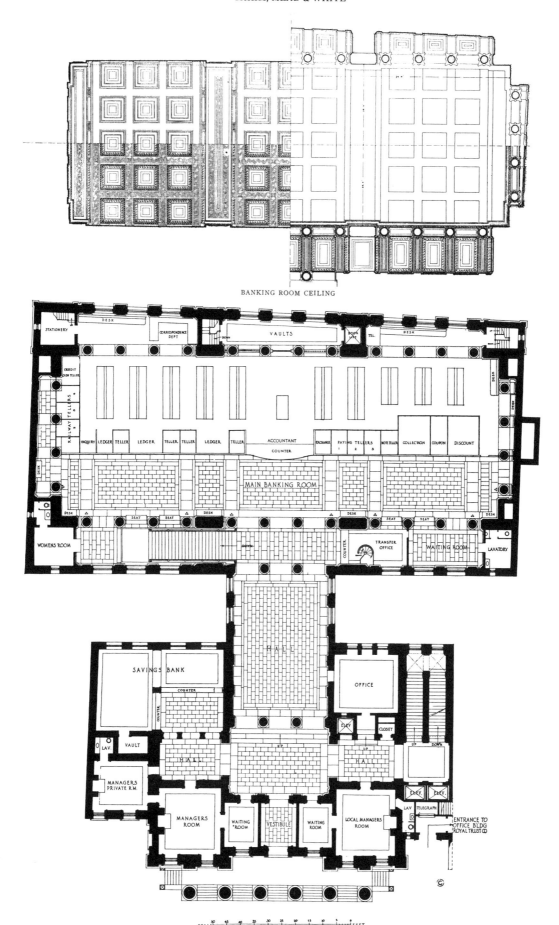

BANKING ROOM CEILING

BANKING ROOM PLAN
THE BANK OF MONTREAL, MONTREAL, CANADA.
1904

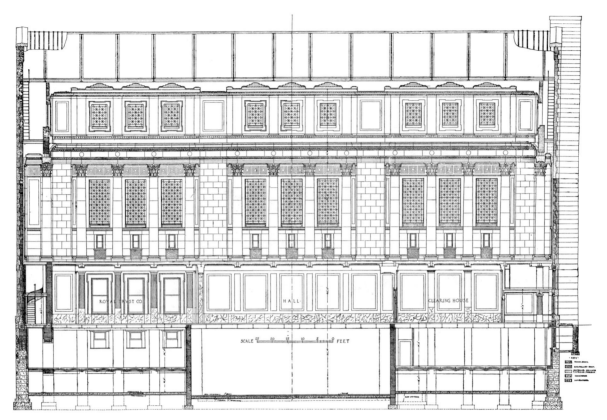

SECTION, MAIN BANKING ROOM

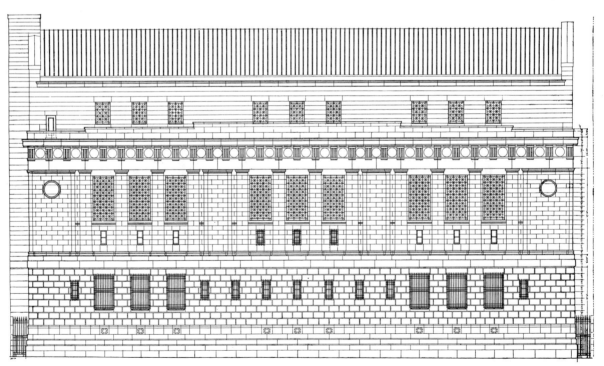

CRAIG STREET ELEVATION

THE BANK OF MONTREAL, MONTREAL, CANADA.

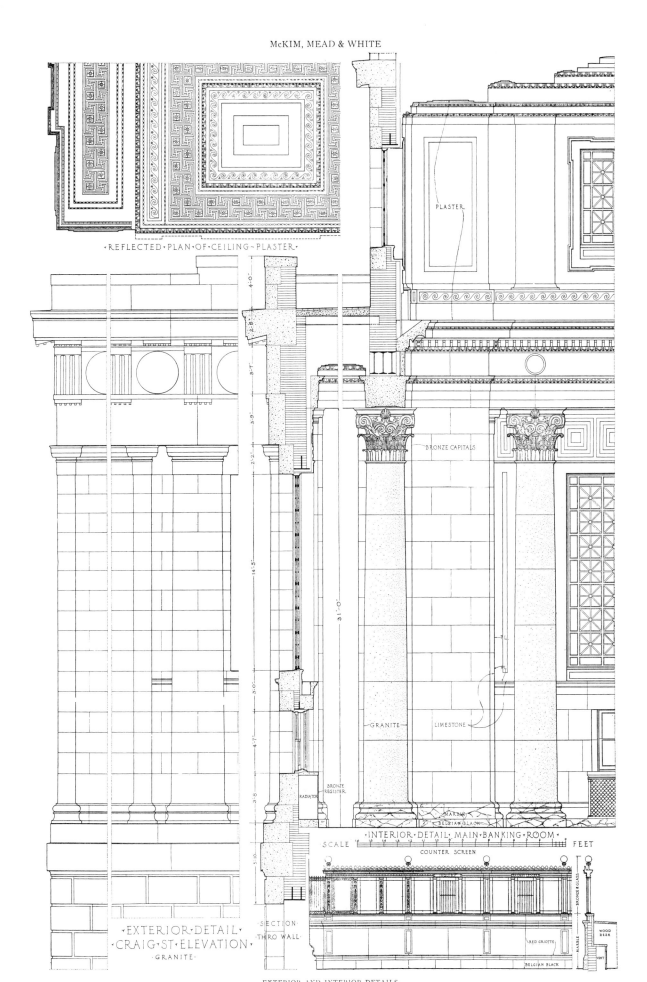

·REFLECTED·PLAN·OF·CEILING·PLASTER·

PLASTER

BRONZE CAPITALS

GRANITE   LIMESTONE

BRONZE
RADIATOR   REGISTER

MARBLE
BELGIAN BLACK

·INTERIOR·DETAIL·MAIN·BANKING·ROOM·

SCALE ⊢⊢⊢⊢⊢⊢⊢⊢⊢⊢ FEET

COUNTER SCREEN

BRONZE & GLASS

RED GRIOTTE

WOOD
DESK

MARBLE

BELGIAN BLACK

VENT

·EXTERIOR·DETAIL·
·CRAIG·ST·ELEVATION·
·GRANITE·

·SECTION·
·THRO WALL·

4'-0" 2'-8" 3'-7" 3'-9" 2'-2" 14'-5" 31'-0" 3'-0" 4'-7" 3'-8" 5'-10"

EXTERIOR AND INTERIOR DETAILS
THE BANK OF MONTREAL, MONTREAL, CANADA.
1904

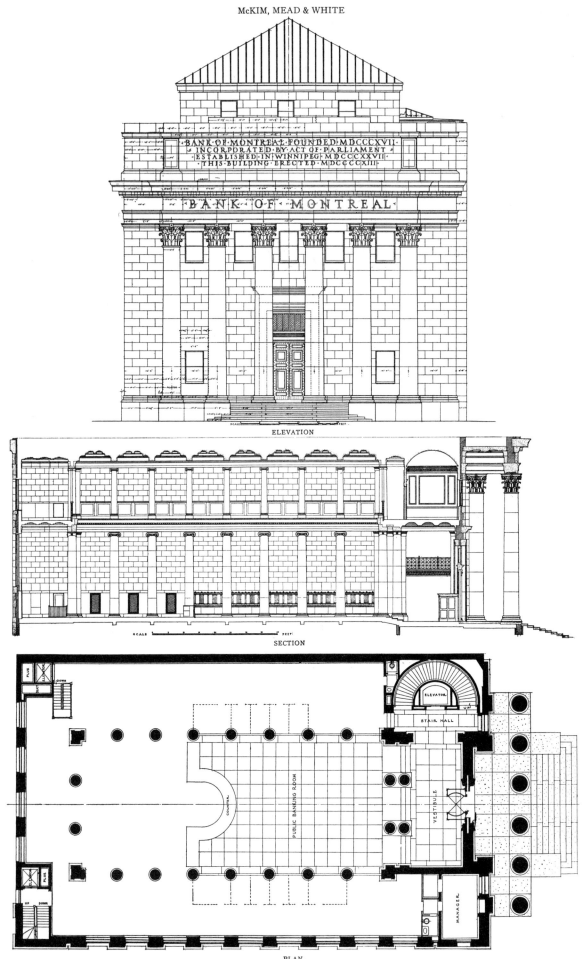

McKIM, MEAD & WHITE

BANK·OF·MONTREAL·FOUNDED·MDCCCXVII
INCORPORATED·BY·ACT·OF·PARLIAMENT
ESTABLISHED·IN·WINNIPEG·MDCCCXXVII
THIS·BUILDING·ERECTED·MDCCCXIII

BANK · OF · MONTREAL

ELEVATION

SECTION

PLAN
THE BANK OF MONTREAL, WINNIPEG BRANCH.
1911

64

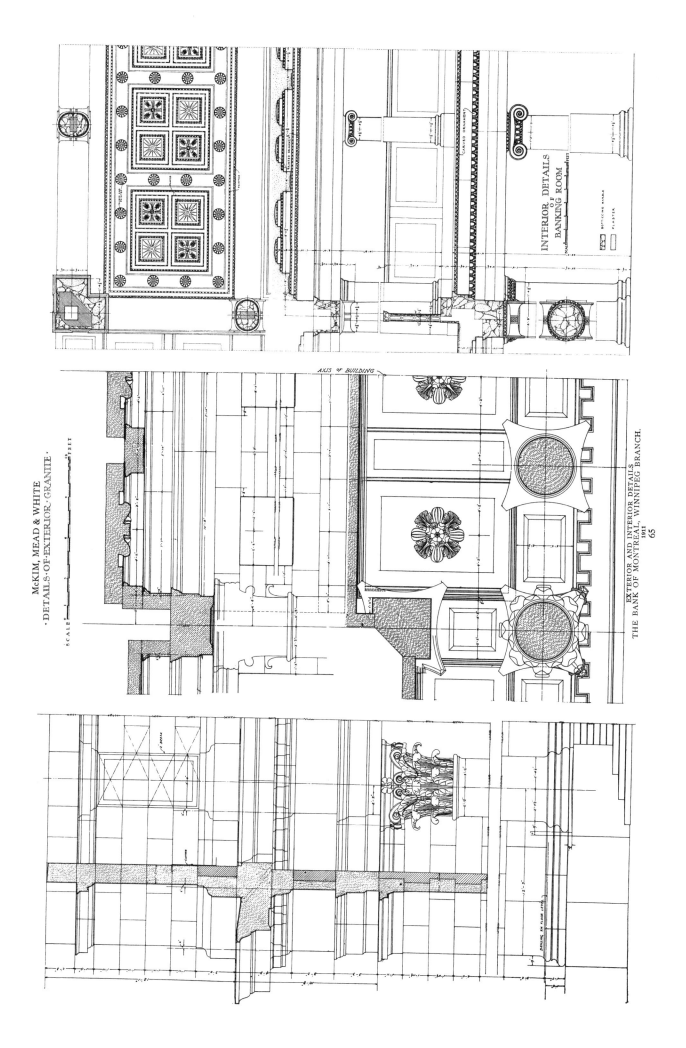

McKIM, MEAD & WHITE
· DETAILS · OF · EXTERIOR · GRANITE ·

SCALE

AXIS OF BUILDING

INTERIOR DETAILS
OF
BANKING ROOM

EXTERIOR AND INTERIOR DETAILS
THE BANK OF MONTREAL, WINNIPEG BRANCH.
1911
65

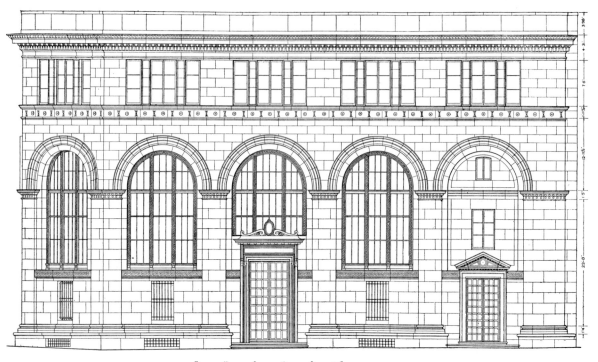

ELEVATION

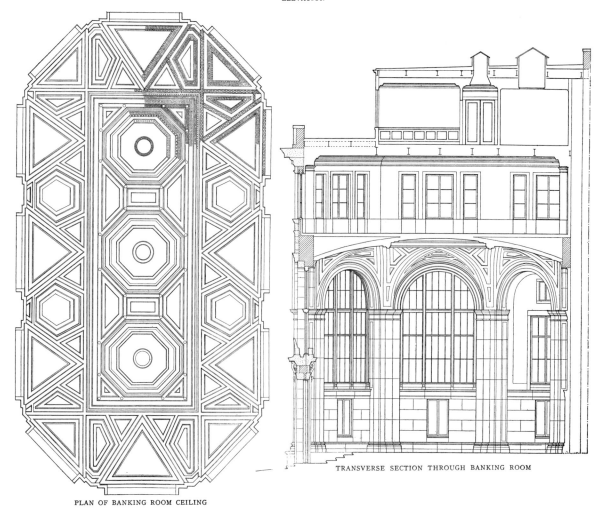

PLAN OF BANKING ROOM CEILING

TRANSVERSE SECTION THROUGH BANKING ROOM

BUILDING FOR THE NEW ENGLAND TRUST CO., BOSTON, MASS.
1906

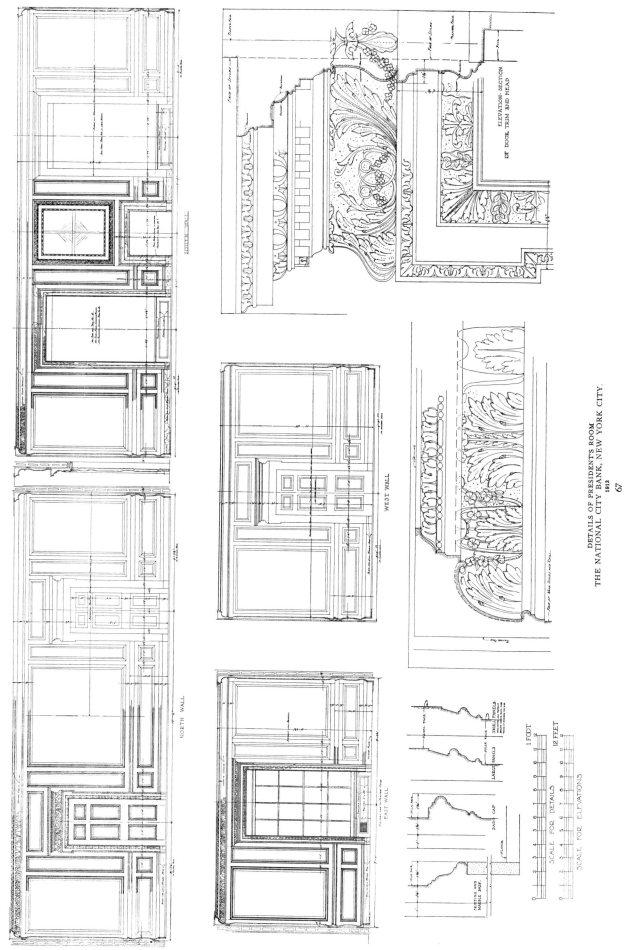

McKIM, MEAD & WHITE

DETAILS OF PRESIDENT'S ROOM
THE NATIONAL CITY BANK, NEW YORK CITY.
1913

67

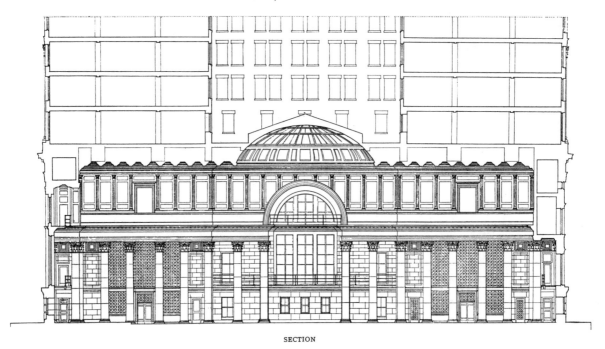

SECTION

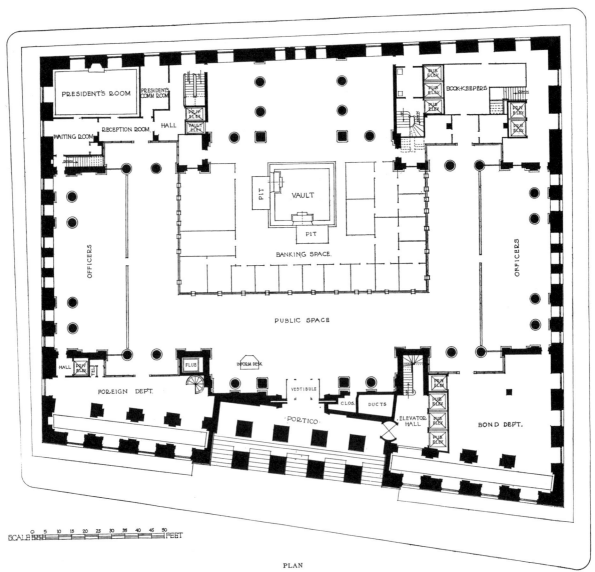

PLAN

THE NATIONAL CITY BANK, NEW YORK CITY.

1909

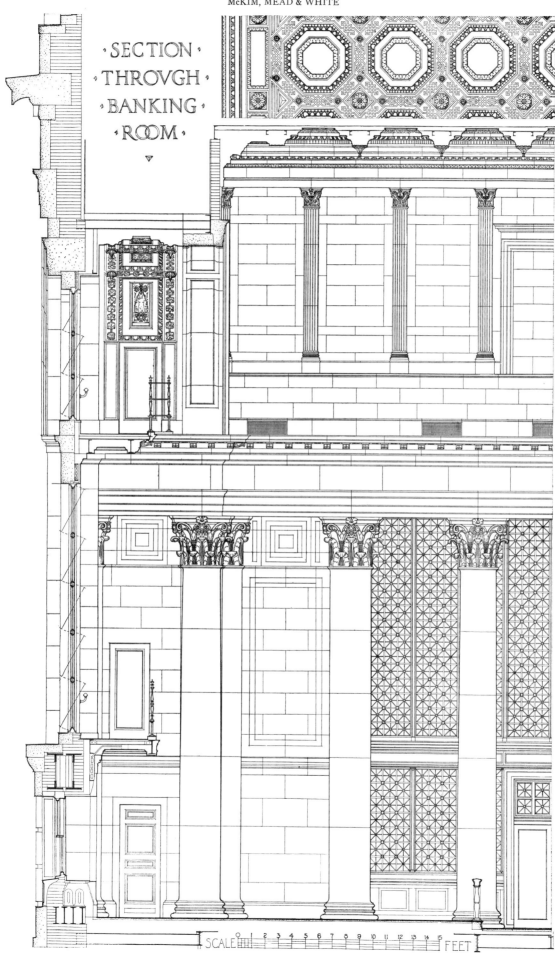

· SECTION ·
· THROVGH ·
· BANKING ·
· ROOM ·

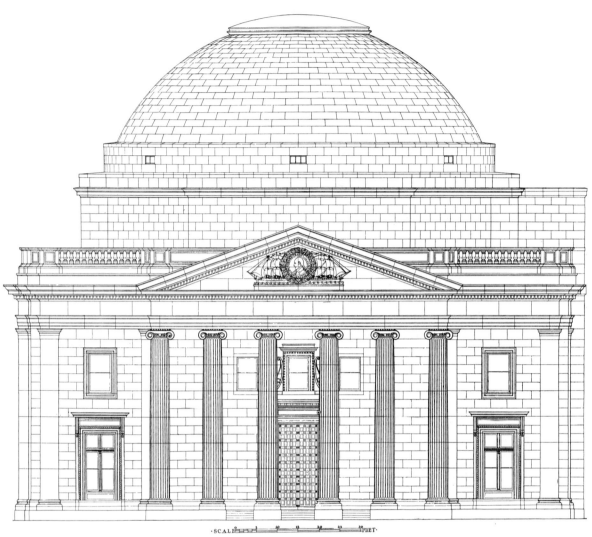

·SCALE············FEET·

ELEVATION

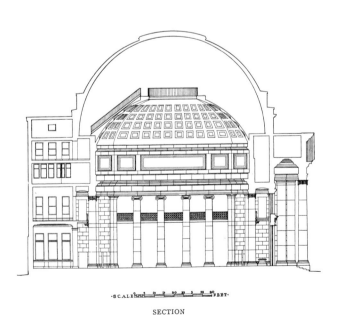

·SCALE············FEET·

SECTION

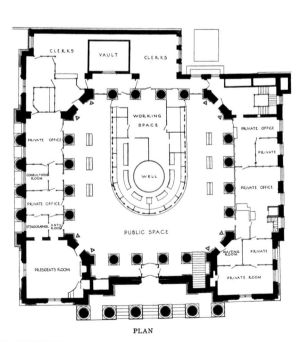

PLAN

THE GIRARD TRUST CO., PHILADELPHIA, PA.
1908

McKIM, MEAD & WHITE

DOOR PANEL

·DETAIL·OF·DOORWAY·

SCALE ⊢⊢⊢⊢⊢⊢⊢⊢⊢⊢⊢⊢⊢⊢⊢⊢ FEET·

MATERIALS, WHITE GEORGIA MARBLE AND CAST BRONZE.
BUILDING FOR THE GIRARD TRUST COMPANY, PHILADELPHIA, PA.
1906

71

SCALE |⊢⊢⊢⊢⊢⊢| FEET

DOWNTOWN BUILDING, COLUMBIA TRUST CO., NEW YORK CITY.
SIDE ELEVATION
1910

DOWNTOWN BUILDING, COLUMBIA TRUST CO., NEW YORK CITY.
EXTERIOR DETAILS, FRONT ELEVATION
1910

SECOND NATIONAL BANK

SCALE FEET

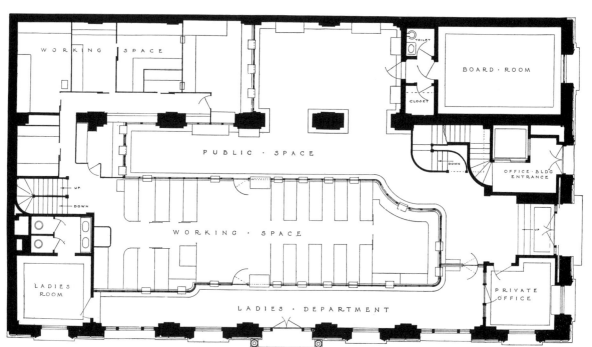

WORKING SPACE

TOILET

BOARD · ROOM

CLOSET

PUBLIC · SPACE

DOWN

OFFICE · BLDG
ENTRANCE

UP

DOWN

UP

WORKING · SPACE

PRIVATE
OFFICE

LADIES
ROOM

LADIES · DEPARTMENT

THE SECOND NATIONAL BANK, NEW YORK CITY.

1907

McKIM, MEAD & WHITE

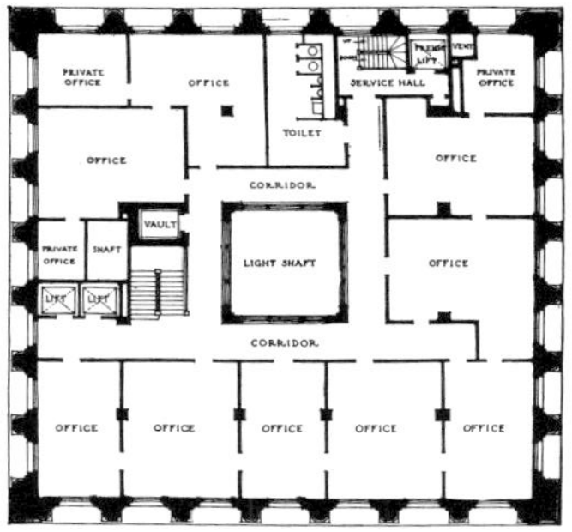

PLAN OF UPPER STORIES

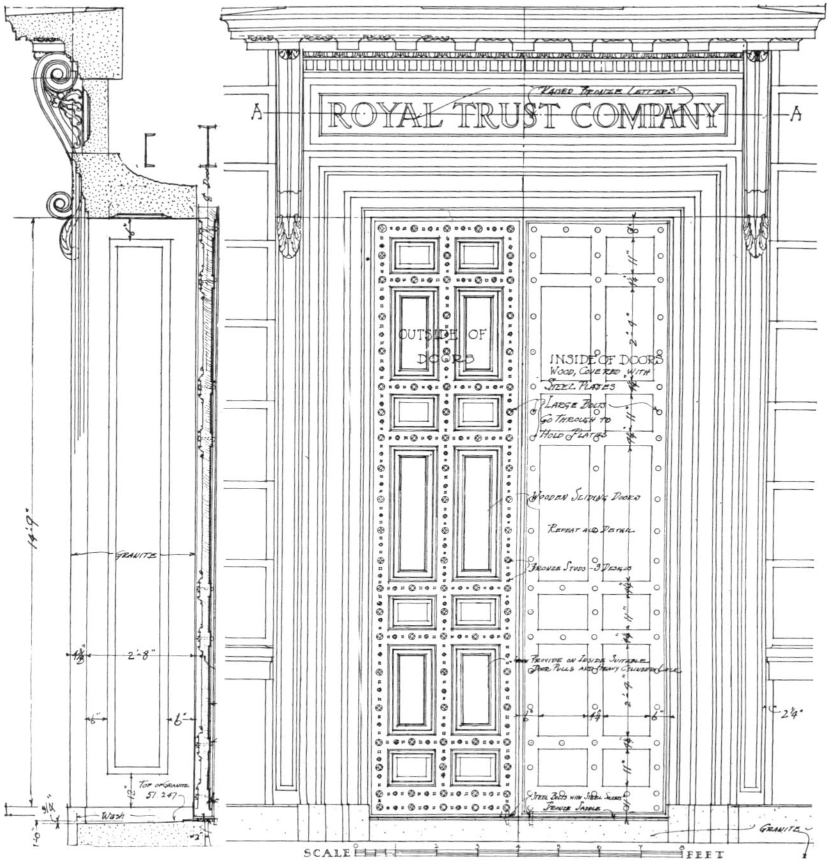

FIRST FLOOR PLAN

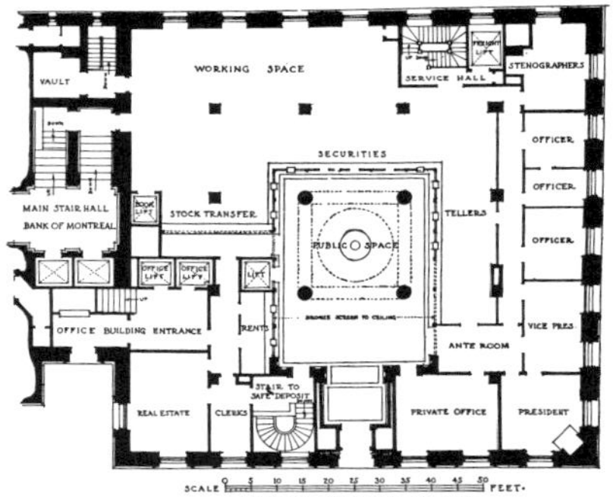

ROYAL TRUST COMPANY

DETAIL OF DOORWAY

ELEVATION

BANK AND OFFICE BUILDING FOR THE ROYAL TRUST COMPANY, MONTREAL, CANADA.
1912

75

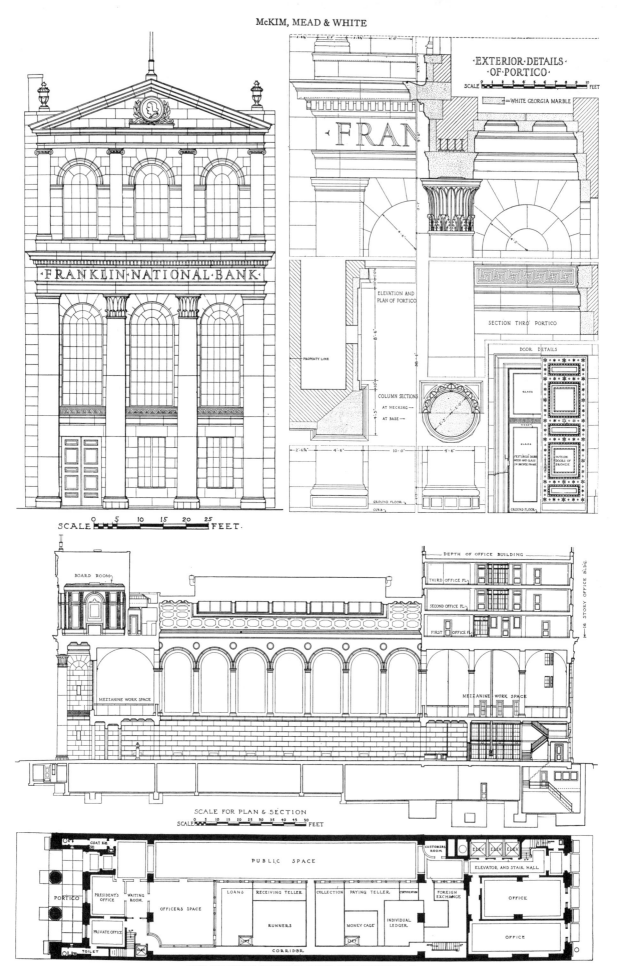

EXTERIOR·DETAILS·
·OF·PORTICO·
SCALE 0 1 2 3 4 5 6 7 8 9 10 FEET

=WHITE GEORGIA MARBLE

·FRANKLIN·NATIONAL·BANK·

SCALE 0 5 10 15 20 25 FEET.

ELEVATION AND PLAN OF PORTICO

SECTION THRO' PORTICO

DOOR DETAILS

PROPERTY LINE

COLUMN SECTIONS
AT NECKING
AT BASE

GROUND FLOOR
CURB

BOARD ROOM

DEPTH OF OFFICE BUILDING
THIRD OFFICE FL.
SECOND OFFICE FL.
FIRST OFFICE FL.

16 STORY OFFICE BLD'G

MEZZANINE WORK SPACE

MEZZANINE WORK SPACE

SCALE FOR PLAN & SECTION
SCALE 0 5 10 15 20 25 30 35 40 45 50 FEET

COAT RM
CUSTOMERS ROOM
ELEV ELEV ELEV
ELEVATOR AND STAIR HALL

PUBLIC SPACE

PORTICO
PRESIDENT'S OFFICE
WAITING ROOM
OFFICERS SPACE
PRIVATE OFFICE
TOILET
LOANS
RECEIVING TELLER
RUNNERS
COLLECTION
PAYING TELLER
MONEY CAGE
INDIVIDUAL LEDGER
CERTIFICATION
FOREIGN EXCHANGE
OFFICE
OFFICE
CORRIDOR

THE FRANKLIN NATIONAL BANK, PHILADELPHIA, PA.
1916

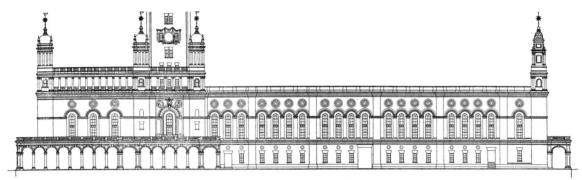

TWENTY-SIXTH STREET ELEVATION

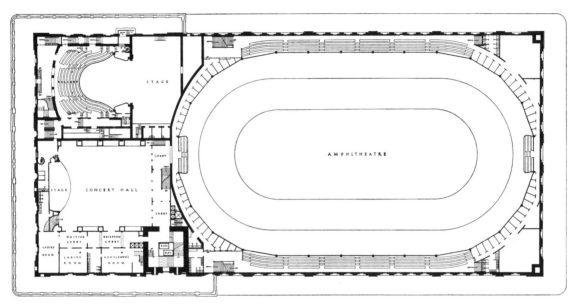

BALCONY FLOOR PLAN

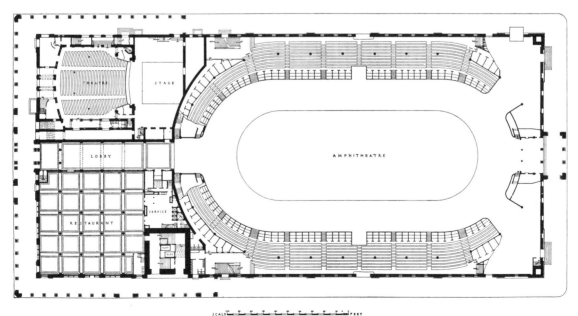

GROUND FLOOR PLAN
MADISON SQUARE GARDEN, NEW YORK CITY.
1891

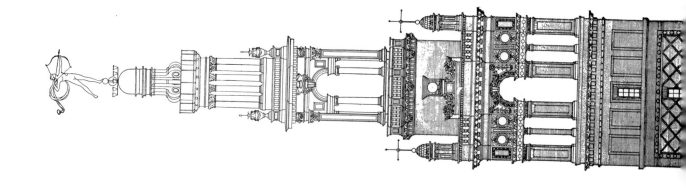

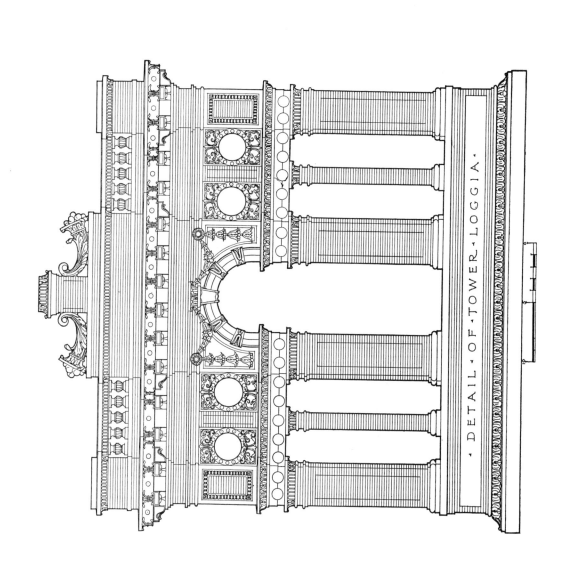

McKIM, MEAD & WHITE

· DETAIL · OF · TOWER · LOGGIA ·

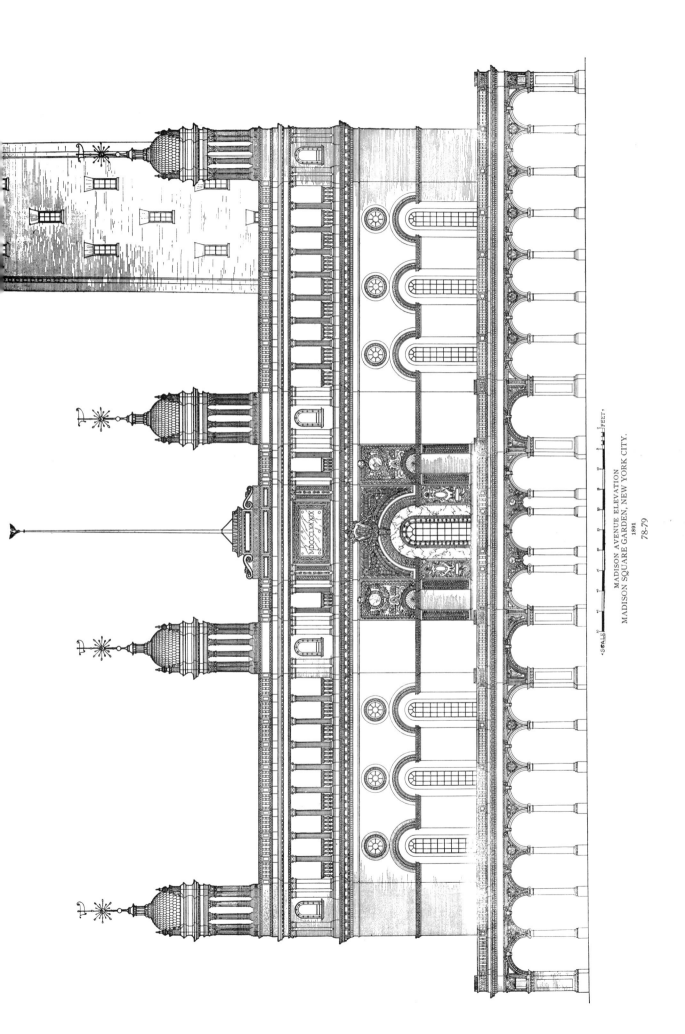

MADISON AVENUE ELEVATION
MADISON SQUARE GARDEN, NEW YORK CITY.
1891

·SCALE·

FEET·

78-79

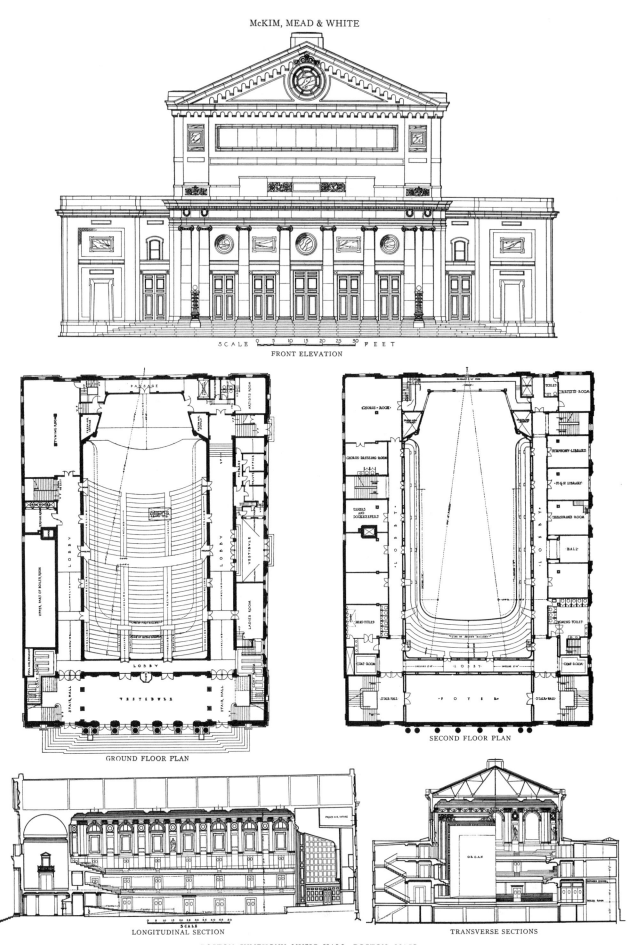

SCALE 0 5 10 15 20 25 30 FEET

FRONT ELEVATION

GROUND FLOOR PLAN

SECOND FLOOR PLAN

SCALE 0 5 10 15 20 25 30 35 40 45 50
LONGITUDINAL SECTION

TRANSVERSE SECTIONS

BOSTON SYMPHONY MUSIC HALL, BOSTON, MASS.
1900

SECTION THROUGH
GABLE CORNICE
ON LINE B-B'

CORNER OF CLEAR STORY GABLE

CENTRAL PORTION OF CLEAR STORY GABLE

SECTION ON
LINE A-A' ABOVE.

SECTION ON LINE C-C'

LEVANTO
MARBLE
INSERTS

CENTER LINE OF FACADE

GLASS

GLASS   GLASS

GLASS

GLASS

SECTION ON CENTER LINE

SCALE

THE BOSTON SYMPHONY MUSIC HALL, BOSTON, MASS.
EXTERIOR DETAILS, FRONT ELEVATION
1900

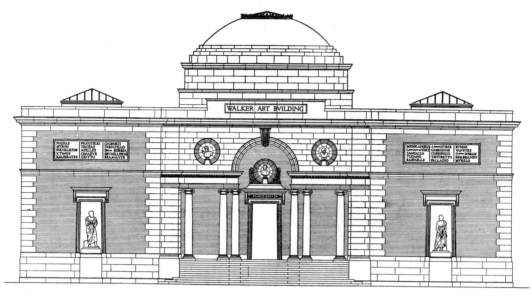

WALKER ART BVILDING

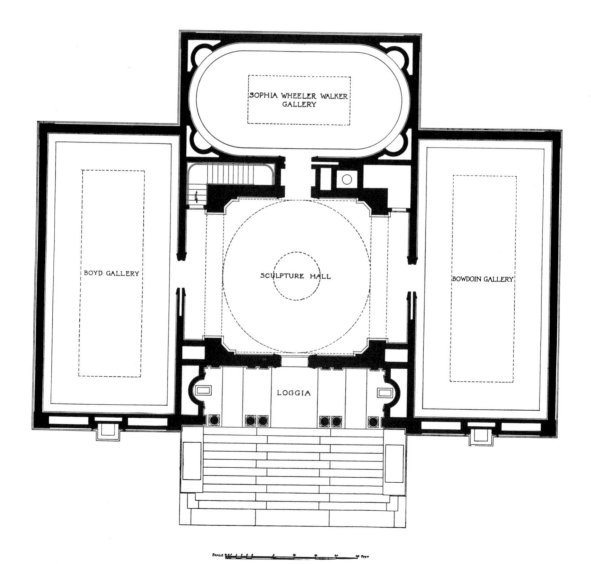

SOPHIA WHEELER WALKER
GALLERY

BOYD GALLERY

SCVLPTVRE HALL

BOWDOIN GALLERY

LOGGIA

WALKER ART GALLERY, BOWDOIN COLLEGE, BRUNSWICK, MAINE.
1893

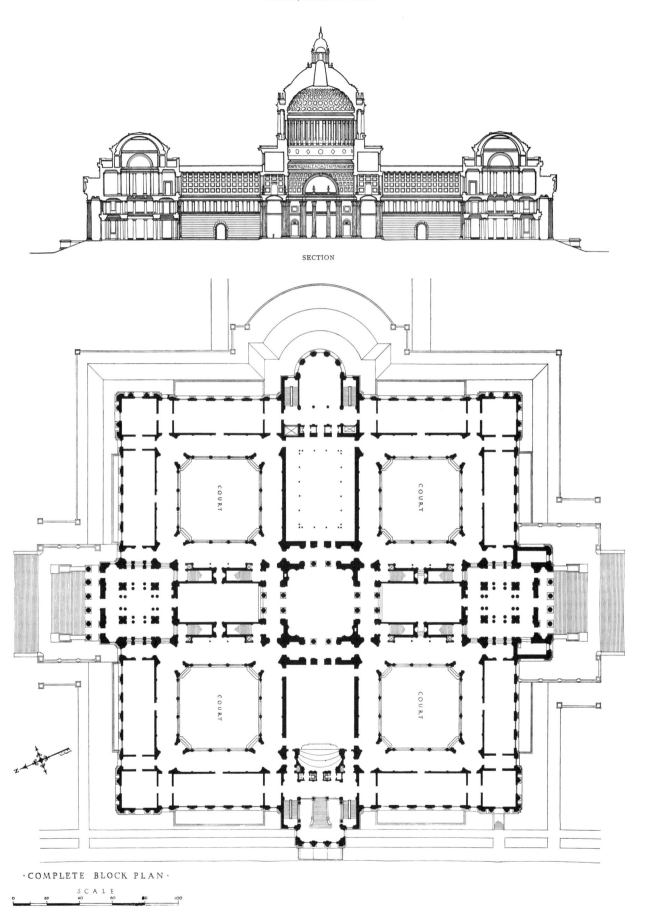

SECTION

·COMPLETE BLOCK PLAN·

SCALE

0   20   40   60   80   100

THE BROOKLYN INSTITUTE OF ARTS AND SCIENCES.
BEGUN 1897

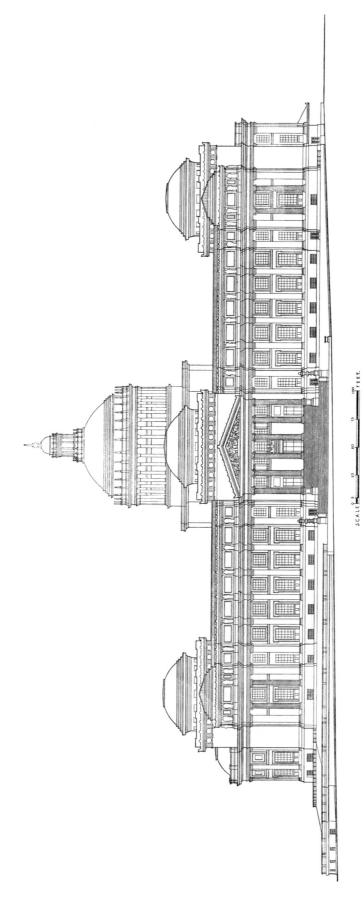

McKIM, MEAD & WHITE

NORTH ELEVATION OF COMPLETED SCHEME
BROOKLYN INSTITUTE OF ARTS AND SCIENCES.
BEGUN 1897

SCALE 0 5   25   50   75   100
                              FEET.

84

ACROTERION
AT APEX
OF PEDIMENT

BASE OF DOME

UPPER CORNICE
CENTRAL PORTION

SOFFIT OF ABOVE CORNICE

MAIN ENTRANCE
DOORWAY

DETAILS OF

NORTH PORTICO

SCALE

MATERIAL~INDIANA LIMESTONE

BRONZE

GRANITE

EXTERIOR DETAILS
BROOKLYN INSTITUTE OF ARTS AND SCIENCES.
1897

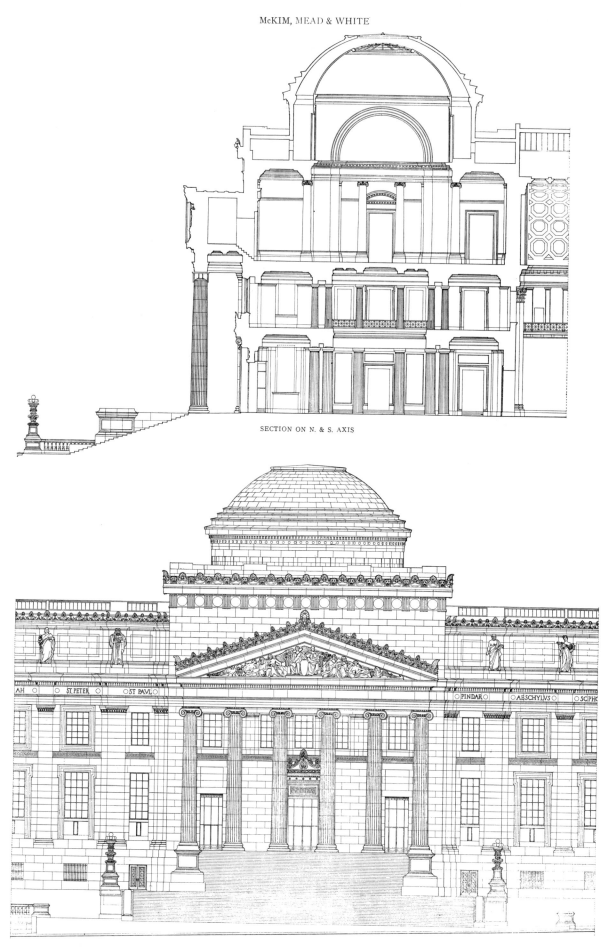

SECTION ON N. & S. AXIS

SCALE ⁵⁰ ⁴⁰ ³⁰ ²⁰ ¹⁰ ⁰ FEET

CENTRAL PORTION, NORTH ELEVATION
THE BROOKLYN INSTITUTE OF ARTS AND SCIENCES.
BEGUN 1897

86

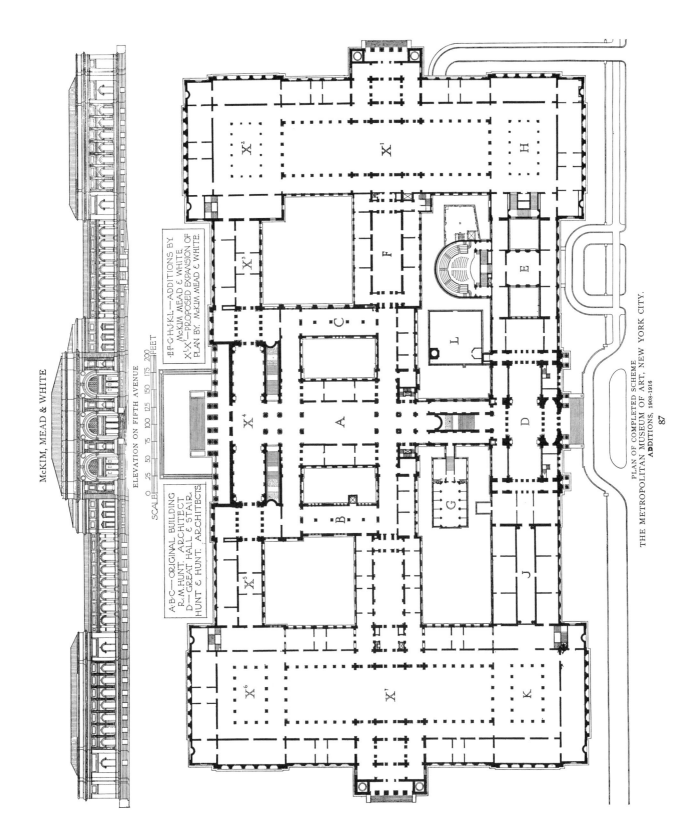

McKIM, MEAD & WHITE

ELEVATION ON FIFTH AVENUE

SCALE 0 25 50 75 100 125 150 175 200 FEET

A·B·C—ORIGINAL BUILDING
R·M·HUNT, ARCHITECT
D—GREAT HALL & STAIR.
HUNT & HUNT, ARCHITECTS.

B·F·G·H·J·K·L—ADDITIONS BY
McKIM MEAD & WHITE.
X¹·X⁷—PROPOSED EXPANSION OF
PLAN BY. McKIM MEAD & WHITE.

X²   X¹   H

X³   F

X⁴   A   C   L   E   D

B   G

X⁵   X⁶   X⁷   J   K

PLAN OF COMPLETED SCHEME
THE METROPOLITAN MUSEUM OF ART, NEW YORK CITY.
ADDITIONS, 1908-1916

87

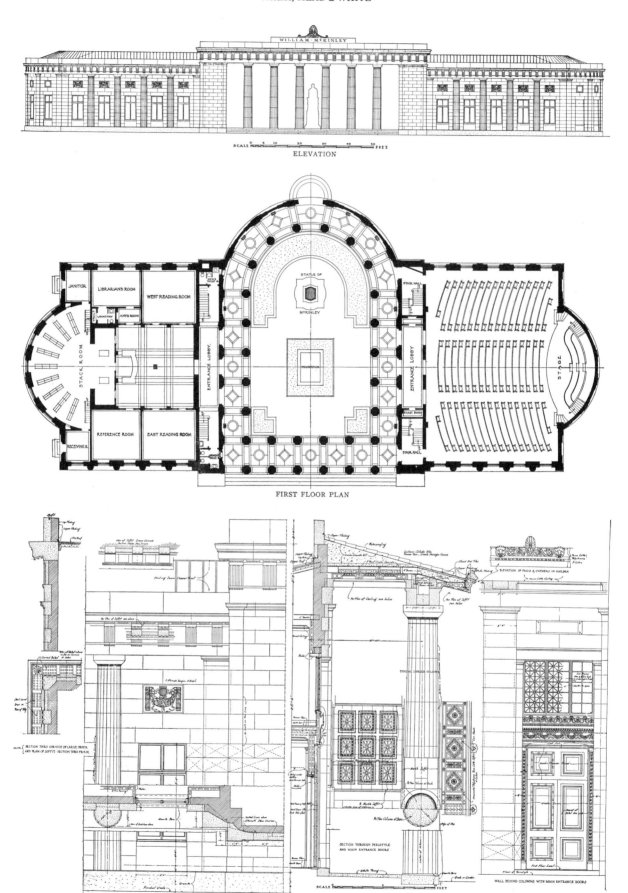

WILLIAM·McKINLEY

ELEVATION

FIRST FLOOR PLAN

EXTERIOR DETAILS - GRANITE, WHITE GEORGIA MARBLE, POLYCHROME TERRA COTTA, ETC.

THE NATIONAL McKINLEY BIRTHPLACE MEMORIAL, NILES, OHIO.

1915

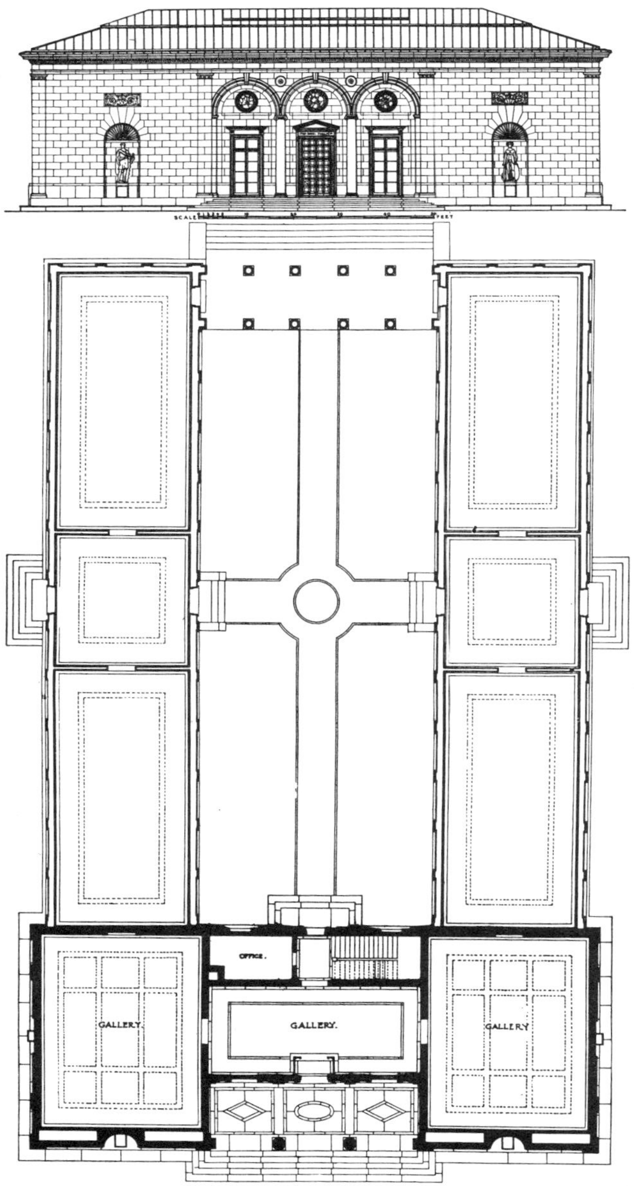

McKIM, MEAD & WHITE

PRO·BONO·

SECTION·THRU·DOORWAY

SECTION·THRU·ARCH·

GALLERY

GALLERY

GALLERY

GALLERY

OFFICE

ART GALLERY FOR MR. JOSEPH G. BUTLER, JR., YOUNGSTOWN, OHIO.

1917

89

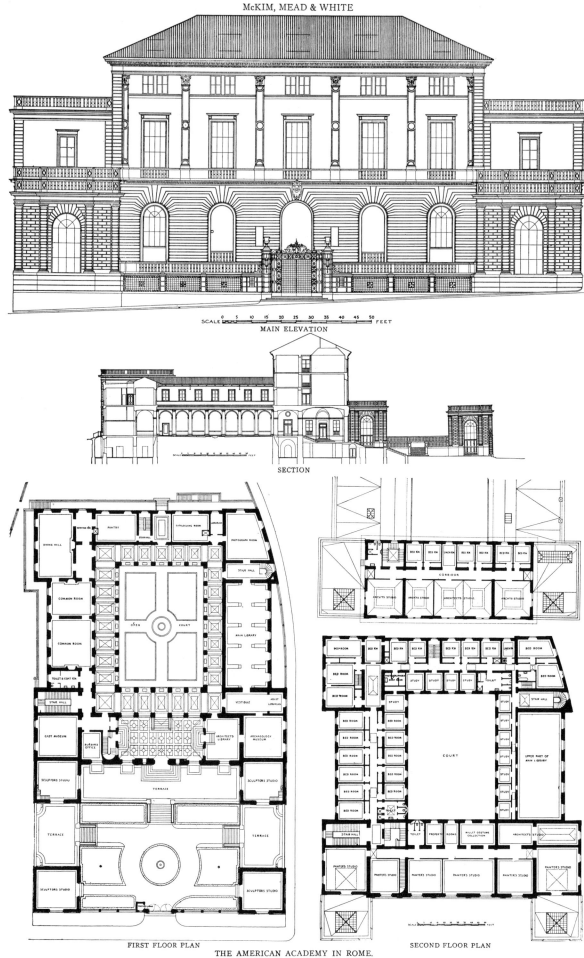

McKIM, MEAD & WHITE

MAIN ELEVATION

SECTION

FIRST FLOOR PLAN

SECOND FLOOR PLAN

THE AMERICAN ACADEMY IN ROME.
1913

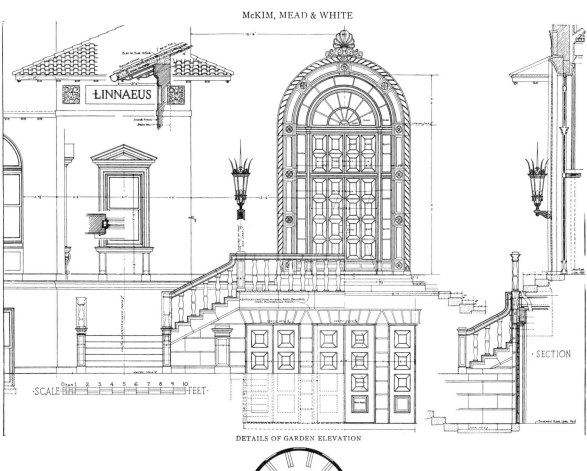

DETAILS OF GARDEN ELEVATION

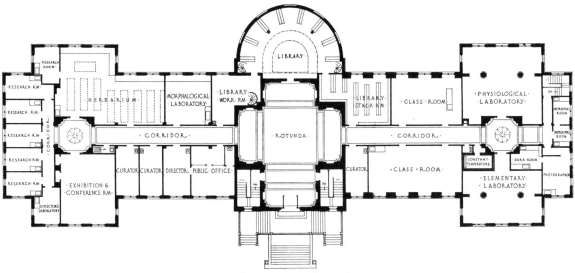

FIRST FLOOR PLAN

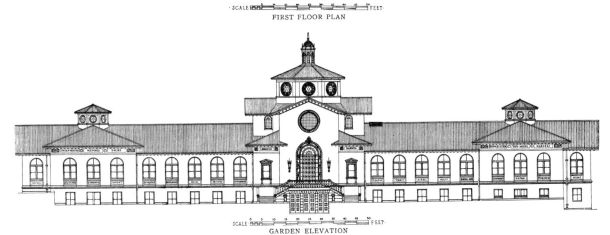

GARDEN ELEVATION

BOTANICAL MUSEUM OF THE BROOKLYN INSTITUTE OF ARTS AND SCIENCES.

1917

McKIM, MEAD & WHITE

SCALE _____ FEET
ELEVATION OF CENTRAL PORTION NOW BUILT

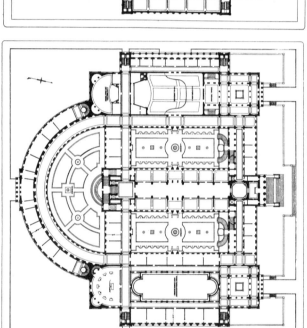

SECOND FLOOR PLAN

BASEMENT PLAN

SCALE _____ FEET
MAIN FLOOR PLAN
THE MINNEAPOLIS MUSEUM OF FINE ARTS.
MINNEAPOLIS, MINNESOTA.
1913

92

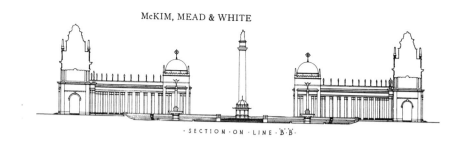

· S E C T I O N · O N · L I N E · B-B ·

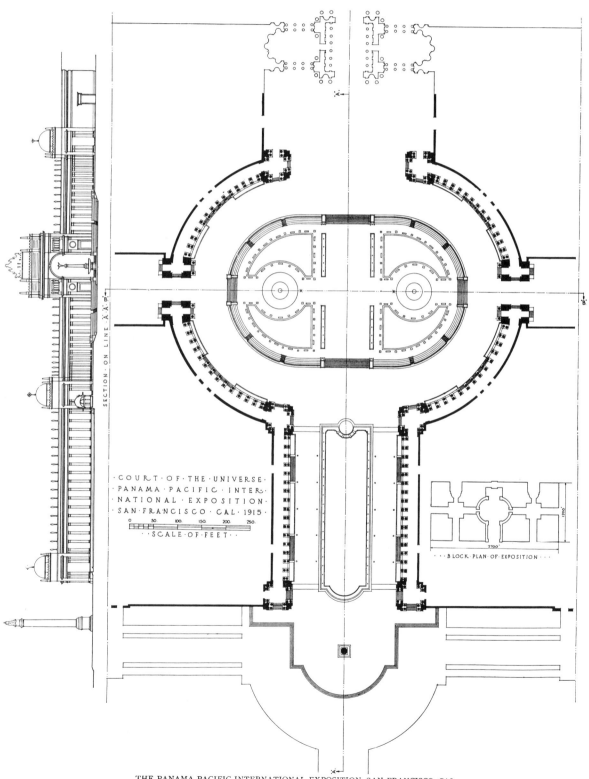

· C O U R T · O F · T H E · U N I V E R S E ·
P A N A M A · P A C I F I C · I N T E R-
N A T I O N A L · E X P O S I T I O N ·
S A N · F R A N C I S C O · C A L · 1 9 1 5 ·

0 50 100. 150. 200. 250.
· S C A L E · O F · F E E T ·

· B L O C K · P L A N · O F · E X P O S I T I O N ·

THE PANAMA PACIFIC INTERNATIONAL EXPOSITION, SAN FRANCISCO, CAL.

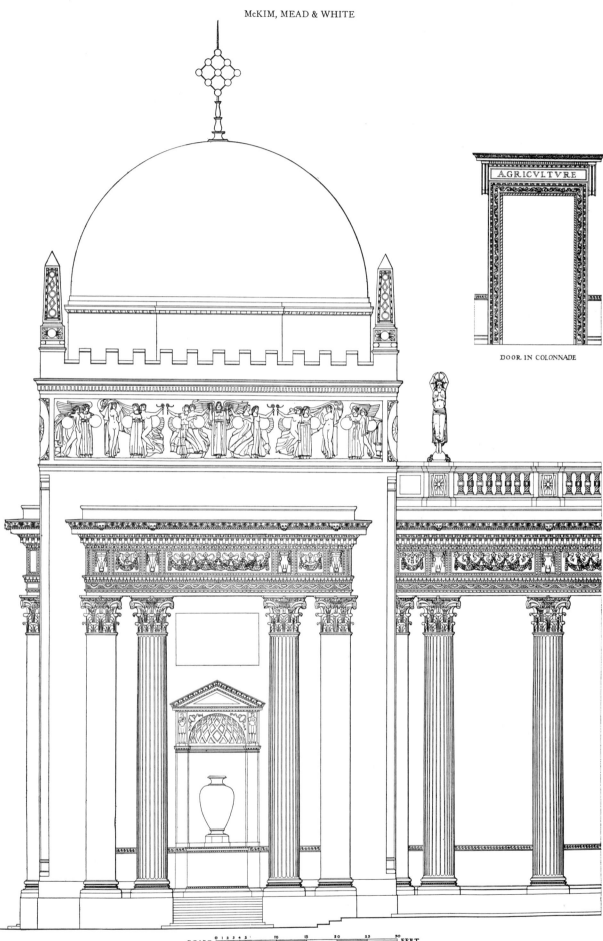

AGRICVLTVRE

DOOR IN COLONNADE

SCALE 0 1 2 3 4 5   10   15   20   25   30 FEET
THIS WORK WAS EXECUTED IN ARTIFICIAL TRAVERTINE, CAST AND PLASTIC, AND DECORATED WITH COLOR.
THE PANAMA PACIFIC INTERNATIONAL EXPOSITION, SAN FRANCISCO, CAL.
DETAIL OF PAVILION AND COLONNADE IN COURT OF THE UNIVERSE.
1915

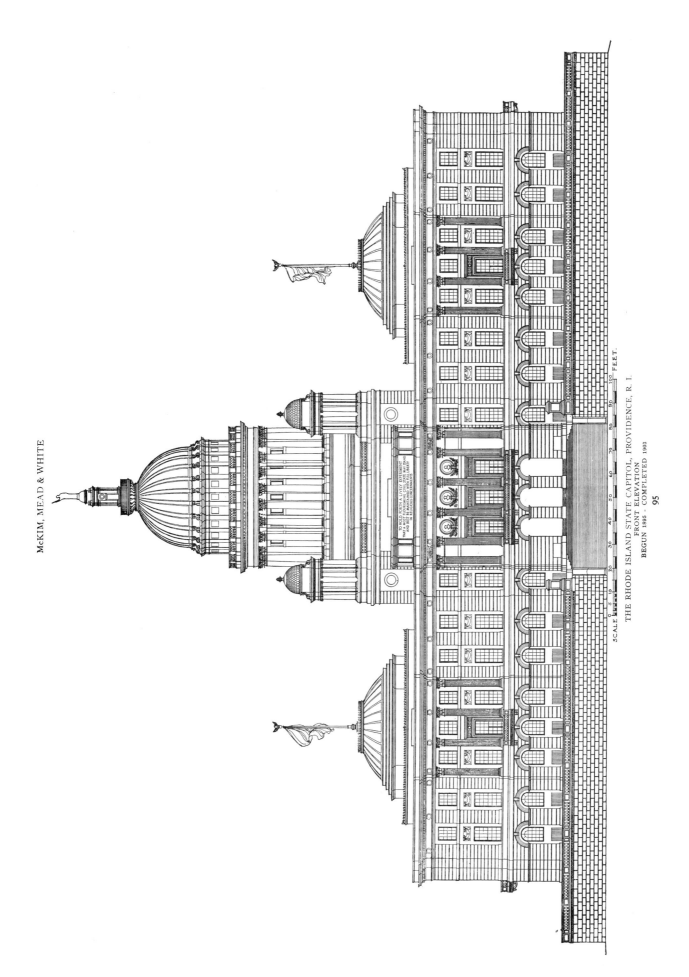

McKIM, MEAD & WHITE

TO HOLD FORTH A LIVELY EXPERIMENT
THAT A MOST FLOURISHING CIVIL STATE MAY STAND
AND BEST BE MAINTAINED WITH FULL LIBERTY
IN RELIGIOUS CONCERNMENTS

SCALE

0 5 10 20 30 40 50 60 70 80 90 100 FEET.

THE RHODE ISLAND STATE CAPITOL, PROVIDENCE, R. I.
FRONT ELEVATION
BEGUN 1895 - COMPLETED 1903

95

McKIM, MEAD & WHITE

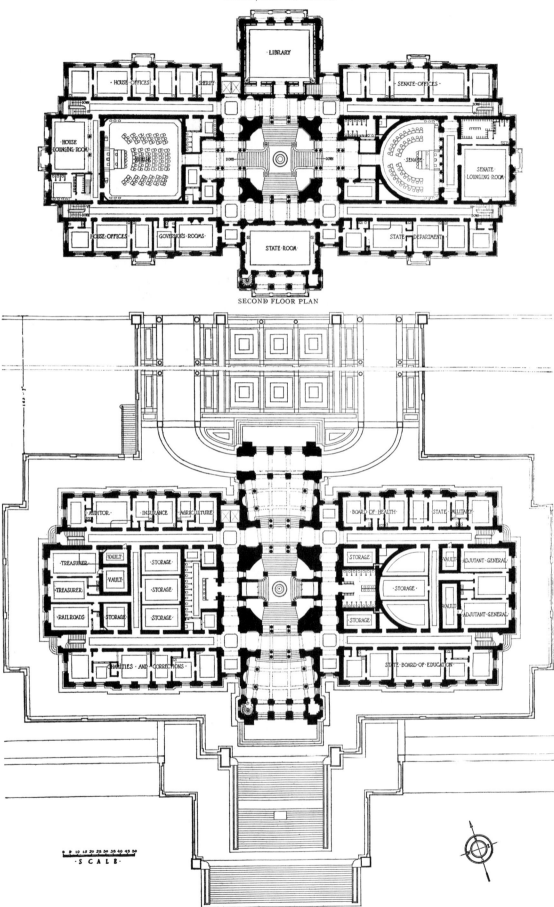

SECOND FLOOR PLAN

FIRST FLOOR PLAN
RHODE ISLAND STATE CAPITOL, PROVIDENCE, R. I.
BEGUN 1895 - COMPLETED 1903

96

THE RHODE ISLAND STATE CAPITOL, PROVIDENCE, R. I.
SECTION THROUGH ROTUNDA
1895 - 1903

PLAN OF CORNER

GRANITE

SECTION·THRO·PORTICO·
·ON·CENTER·LINE·

·DETAIL·OF·CENTRAL·PORTION·OF·SOUTH·ELEVATION·

SCALE FEET

THE RHODE ISLAND STATE CAPITOL, PROVIDENCE, R. I.

1895 - 1903

McKIM, MEAD & WHITE

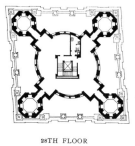

28TH FLOOR

32ND FLOOR

36TH FLOOR

PLANS OF TOWER

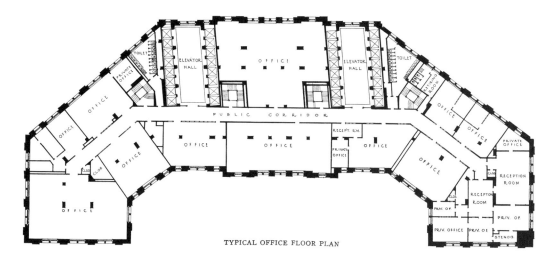

TYPICAL OFFICE FLOOR PLAN

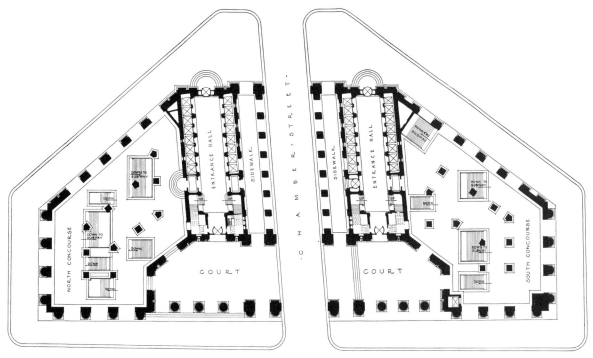

GROUND FLOOR PLAN

SCALE FEET·

THE MUNICIPAL BUILDING, NEW YORK CITY.
1908

99

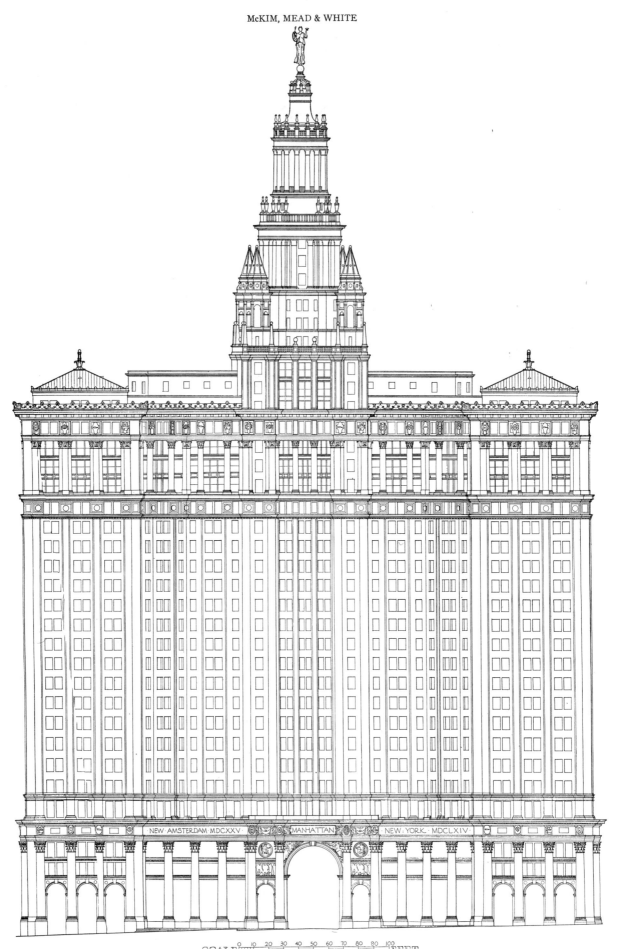

McKIM, MEAD & WHITE

NEW · AMSTERDAM · MDCXXV · MANHATTAN · NEW · YORK · MDCLXIV

SCALE 0 10 20 30 40 50 60 70 80 90 100 FEET

THE MUNICIPAL BUILDING, NEW YORK CITY.
WEST ELEVATION
1908
100

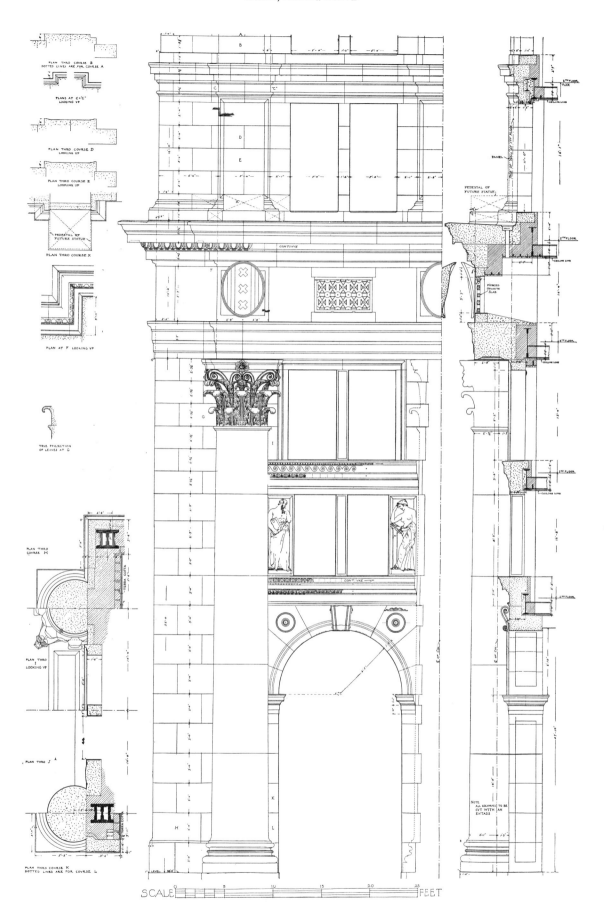

SCALE 0 5 10 15 20 25 FEET

THE MUNICIPAL BUILDING, NEW YORK CITY.
DETAIL OF LOWER STORIES
1908
101

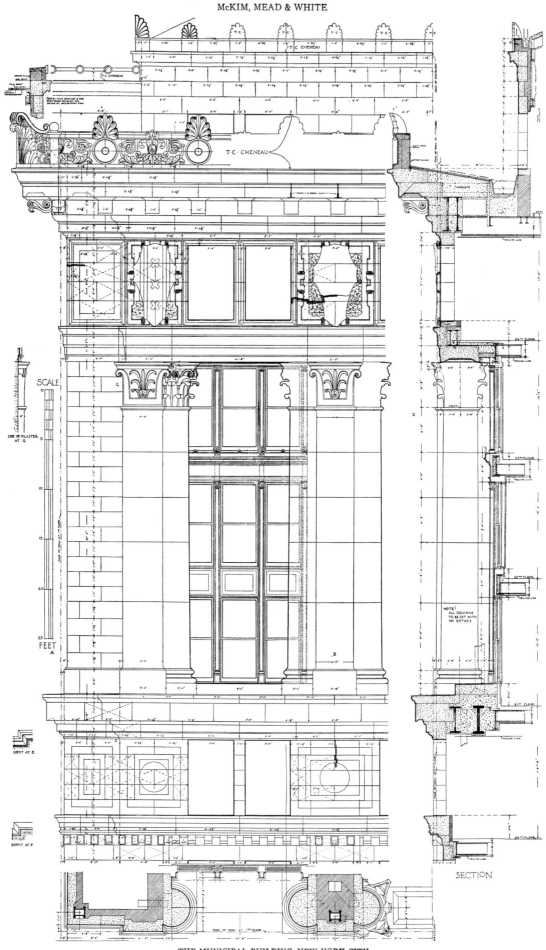

THE MUNICIPAL BUILDING, NEW YORK CITY.
DETAIL OF UPPER STORIES
1908

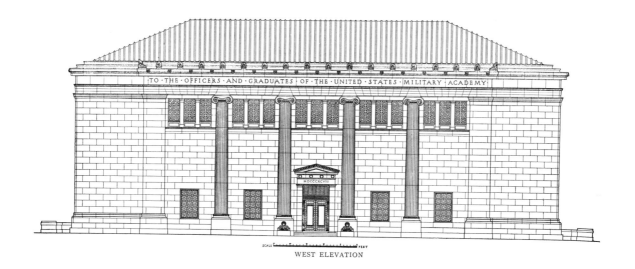

TO · THE · OFFICERS · AND · GRADUATES · OF · THE · UNITED · STATES · MILITARY · ACADEMY

SCALE [   ] FEET

WEST ELEVATION

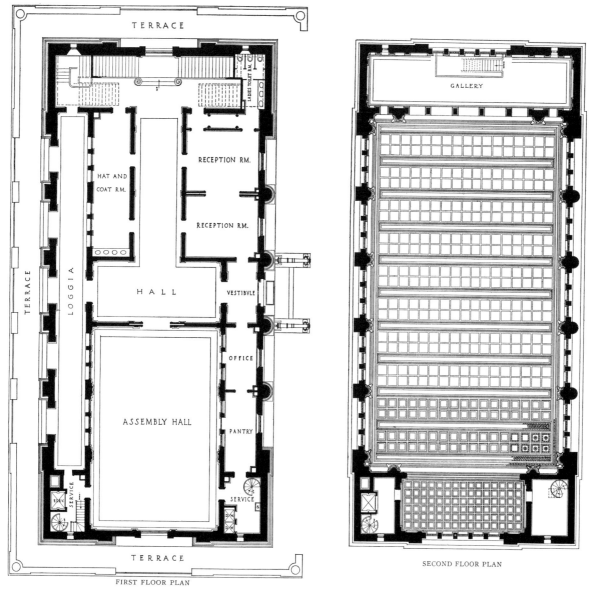

TERRACE

RECEPTION RM.

HAT AND
COAT RM.

RECEPTION RM.

LADIES TOILET RM.

TERRACE

LOGGIA

HALL

VESTIBVLE

OFFICE

ASSEMBLY HALL

PANTRY

SERVICE

SERVICE

TERRACE

FIRST FLOOR PLAN

GALLERY

SECOND FLOOR PLAN

CULLUM MEMORIAL, WEST POINT, N. Y.
1898

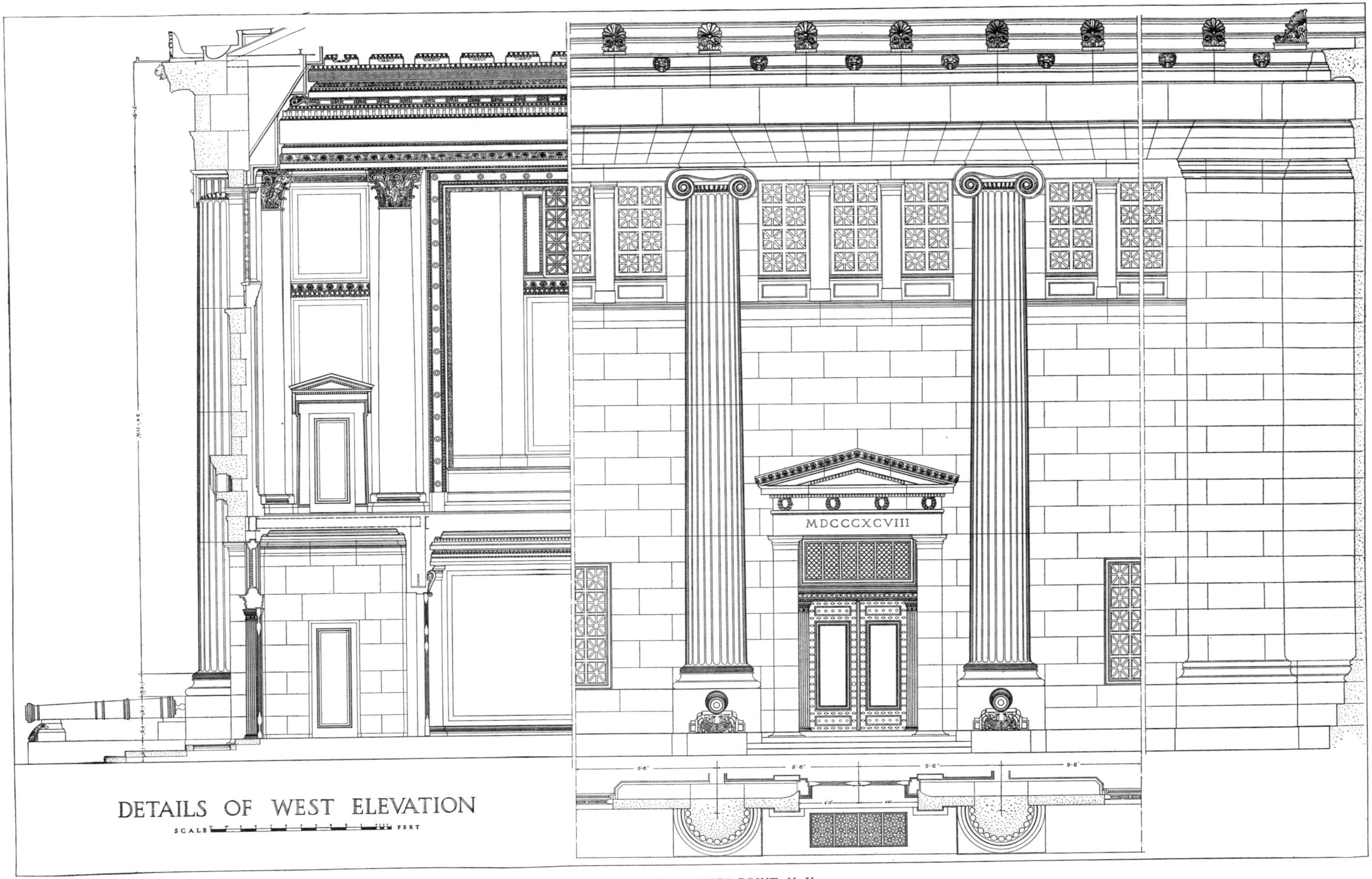

McKIM, MEAD & WHITE

MDCCCXCVIII

DETAILS OF WEST ELEVATION
SCALE

CULLUM MEMORIAL, WEST POINT, N. Y.
1898
104

‹DETAIL OF MAIN ENTRANCE› ‹SECTION›

SCALE |___|___|___|___|___|___|___|___|___||||| FEET

JUDSON MEMORIAL CHURCH, WASHINGTON SQUARE, NEW YORK CITY.
1893

·FRONT ELEVATION·
·MADISON SQVARE PRESBYTERIAN CHVRCH·
·SCALE ¼ INCH EQVALS ONE FOOT·

STREET ELEVATION

PORTICO VESTIBVLE

AVDITORIVM

PVLPIT

VAVLT RM.

VAVLT

PASTOR'S RM.

SEXTON

TEL

DOWN
UP

EXIT

SWITCH AND
BOARD RM.

COVRT

LECTVRE ROOM

CHOIR

CLOS.

PACKING ROOM

DOWN

CHOIR ROOM

HALL

CLOS.

CLOSET

PASSAGE

VESTIBVLE
DOWN

SESSION RM.

DOWN

SCALE 0 5 10 15 20 25 30 35 40 45 50 FEET

PLAN
MADISON SQUARE PRESBYTERIAN CHURCH, NEW YORK CITY.
1906

107

SCALE 0 1 2 3 4 5 FEET

·DETAIL·OF·
·PORTICO·

·BALVSTRADE·

CAPITALS, ENTABLATURE, BALUSTRADE, WINDOW TRIM OF ORNAMENTAL TERRA COTTA, SHAFT OF COLUMN, POLISHED GREEN GRANITE.
BASE, WHITE MARBLE. WALLS, LIGHT BRICK.
MADISON SQUARE PRESBYTERIAN CHURCH, NEW YORK CITY.
1906

·VPPER·
·CORNICE·

·MAIN·DOORWAY·

SCALE 0 1 2 3 4 5 FEET

SECTION

MARBLE·JAMB

WALLS, LIGHT BRICK. CORNICES AND DOOR TRIM, ORNAMENTAL TERRA COTTA MARBLE INSERTS, PAVONAZZO. OAK DOORS WITH IRON STUDS.
MADISON SQUARE PRESBYTERIAN CHURCH, NEW YORK CITY.
1906

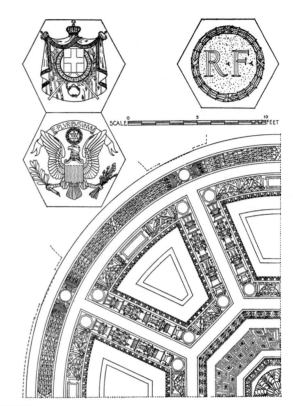

SCALE ⊢━━━━━━━━━━━━━━━━━━━━⊣ FEET
0   5   10

DETAILS OF PLASTER CEILING

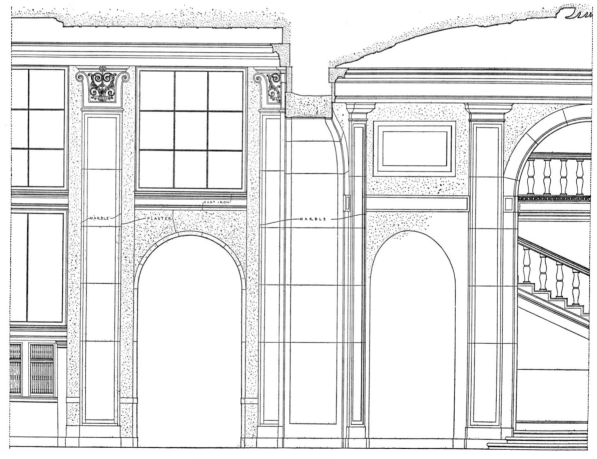

UNITED STATES POSTOFFICE, NEW YORK CITY.
DETAILS OF PUBLIC CORRIDOR, FIRST FLOOR
1913

McKIM, MEAD & WHITE

TERRA COTTA CHENEAU

·DETAIL·OF·ATTIC·

GRANITE

·SCALE·

·EXTERIOR·
·DETAILS·
·OF·THE·
·U·S·POST·
·OFFICE·
·NEW·YORK·N·Y·

GRANITE

·DETAIL·OF·
·ENTRANCES·
·THIRTY·FIRST·&·
·THIRTY·THIRD·ST́S·

·DETAIL·OF·NICHE·   ·SECTION·

CAST·IRON

CAST·IRON

GRANITE

·PLAN·THRU·END·
·OF·COLONNADE·

·SECTION·THRU·COLONNADE·

UNITED STATES POST OFFICE, NEW YORK CITY.
1913
111

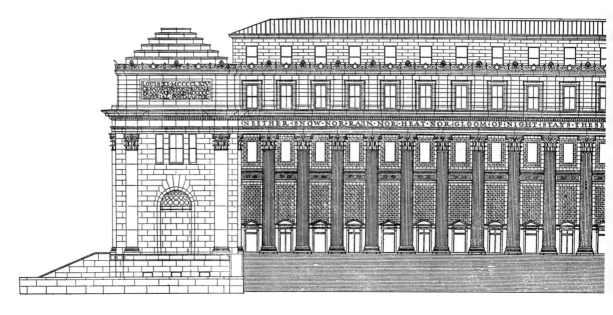

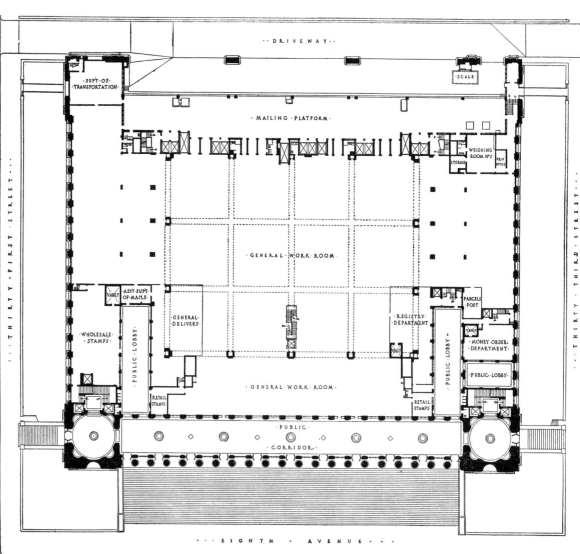

FIRST FLOOR PLAN

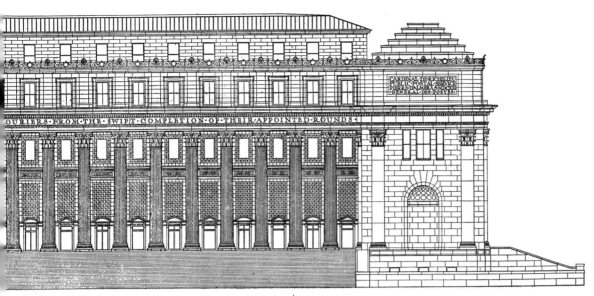

SCALE

FRONT ELEVATION

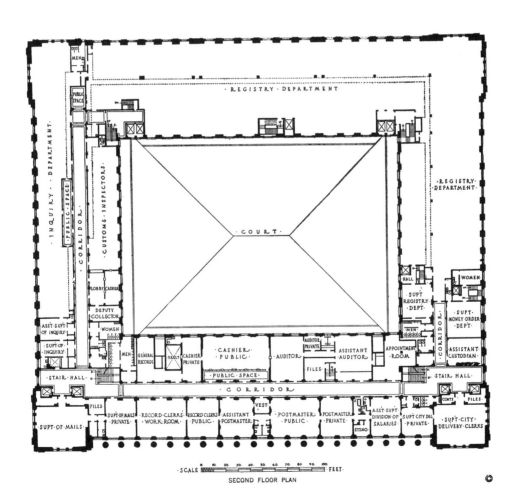

SCALE FEET

SECOND FLOOR PLAN

UNITED STATES POSTOFFICE, NEW YORK CITY.
1913

113

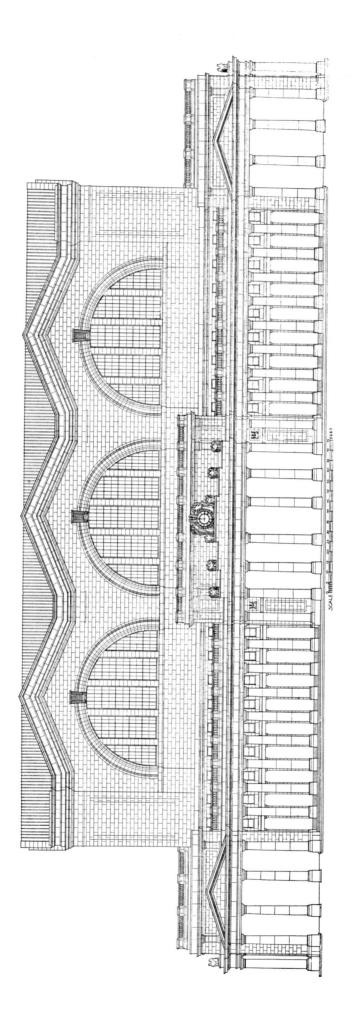

McKIM, MEAD & WHITE

THE PENNSYLVANIA RAILROAD STATION, NEW YORK CITY.
SEVENTH AVENUE ELEVATION
1906-1910

114

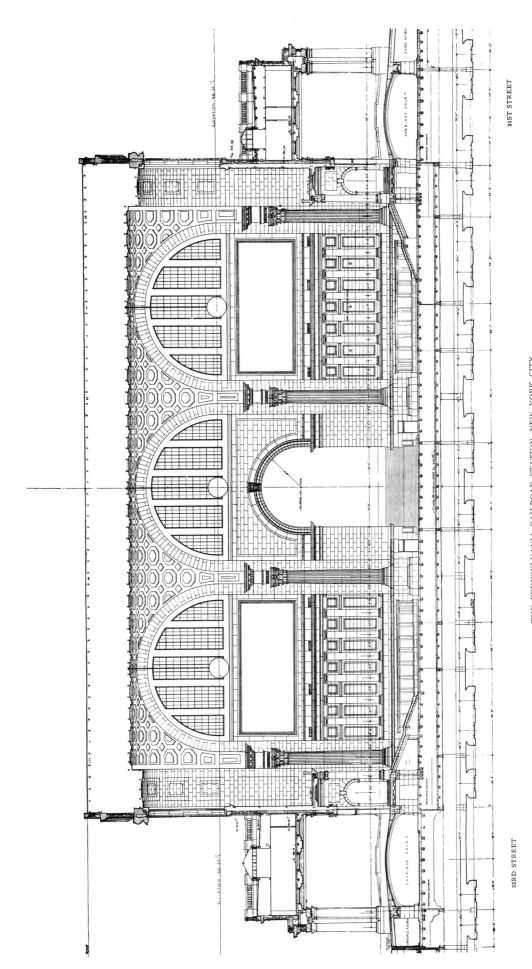

McKIM, MEAD & WHITE

THE PENNSYLVANIA RAILROAD STATION, NEW YORK CITY.
SECTION THROUGH MAIN WAITING ROOM
1906-1910

115

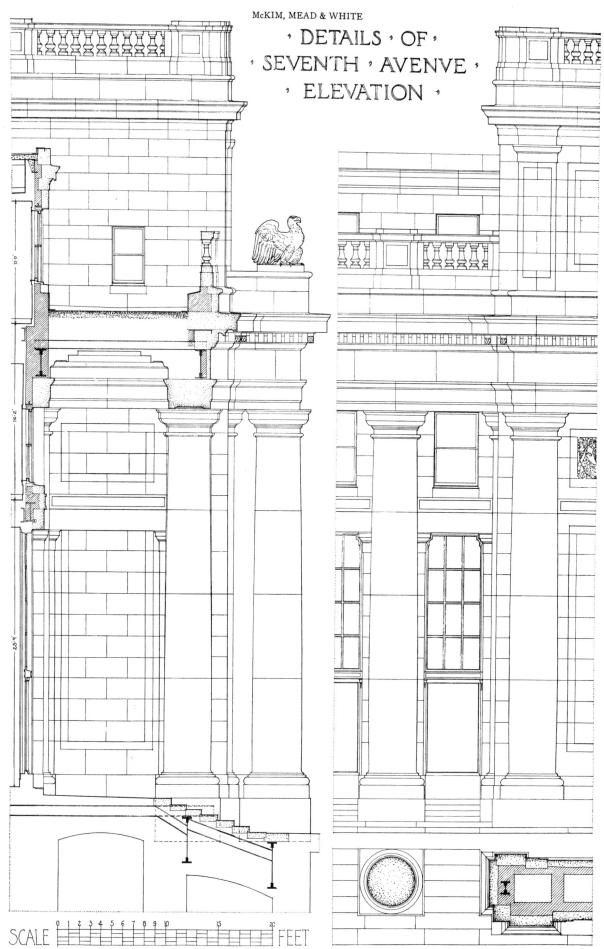

McKIM, MEAD & WHITE

· DETAILS · OF ·
· SEVENTH · AVENVE ·
· ELEVATION ·

SCALE 0 1 2 3 4 5 6 7 8 9 10   15   20 FEET

THE PENNSYLVANIA RAILROAD STATION, NEW YORK CITY.
1906-1910

116

DETAILS
MAIN
WAITING·ROOM

SPRING LINE

SCALE   0 1 2 3 4 5   10   15   20   25   30   FEET

THE PENNSYLVANIA RAILROAD STATION, NEW YORK CITY.
INTERIOR DETAILS
1906-1910

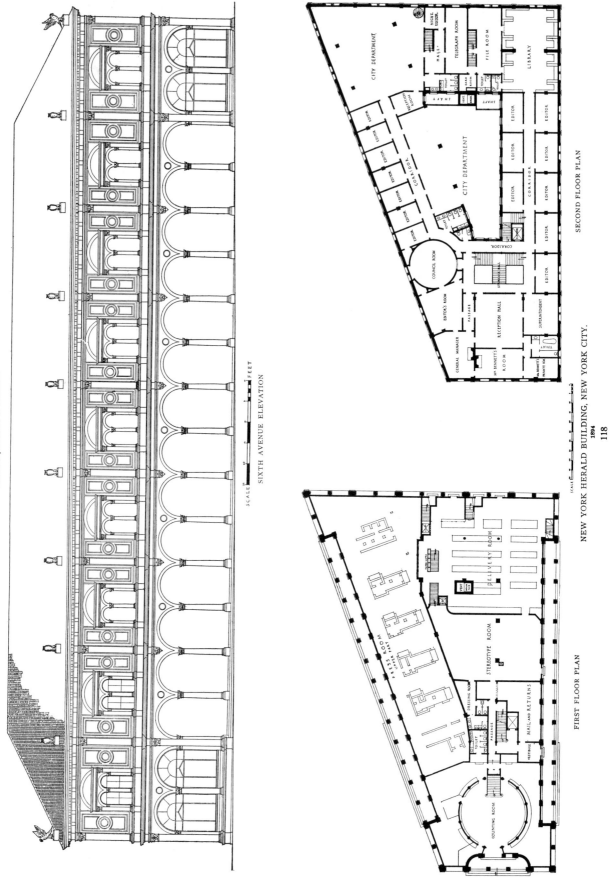

McKIM, MEAD & WHITE

SIXTH AVENUE ELEVATION

SECOND FLOOR PLAN

FIRST FLOOR PLAN

NEW YORK HERALD BUILDING, NEW YORK CITY.
1894

118

McKIM, MEAD & WHITE

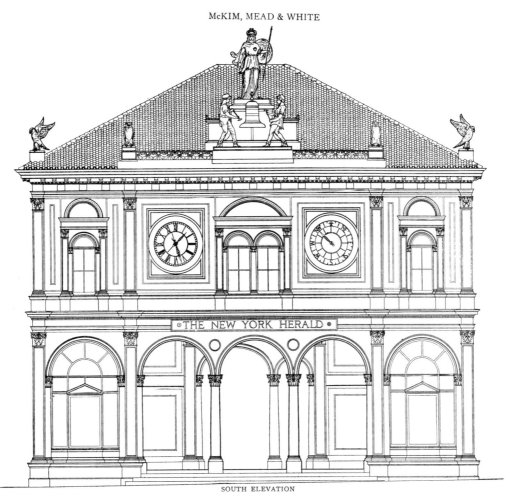

THE NEW YORK HERALD

SOUTH ELEVATION

DETAIL OF BROADWAY FACADE
NEW YORK HERALD BUILDING, NEW YORK CITY.
1894

119

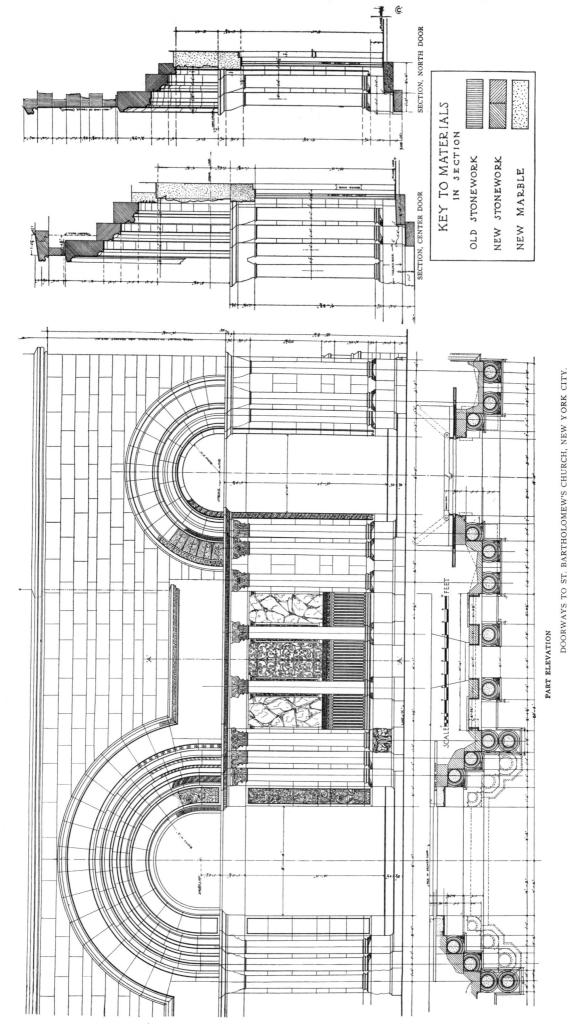

McKIM, MEAD & WHITE

SECTION, NORTH DOOR

SECTION, CENTER DOOR

KEY TO MATERIALS
IN SECTION

OLD STONEWORK

NEW STONEWORK

NEW MARBLE

PART ELEVATION

DOORWAYS TO ST. BARTHOLOMEW'S CHURCH, NEW YORK CITY.

1903

120

SCALE ...... FEET

TERRA COTTA

TERRA COTTA

SGRAFFITO

SCALE ...... FEET

BUCKINGHAM BUILDING. WATERBURY, CONN.
ELEVATION AND DETAILS
1906

SCALE

SIDE ELEVATION

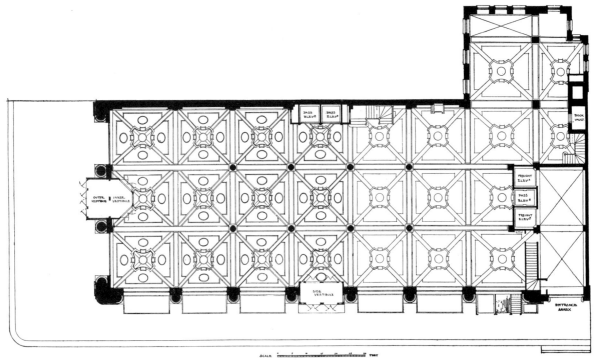

SCALE

FIRST FLOOR PLAN
THE GORHAM BUILDING, NEW YORK CITY.
1906

THE GORHAM BUILDING, NEW YORK CITY.
FIFTH AVENUE ELEVATION
1906

APPLIED BRONZE ORNAMENT

ENTRANCE VESTIBULE SHOWN IN PLAN AND
ELEVATION

SECTION THROUGH WALL

FLOOR PLAN   CEILING PLAN

BRONZE BALCONY RAIL

· SCALE · OF · FEET ·

GRANITE   LIMESTONE

THE GORHAM BUILDING, NEW YORK CITY.
DETAILS OF LOWER STORIES
1906

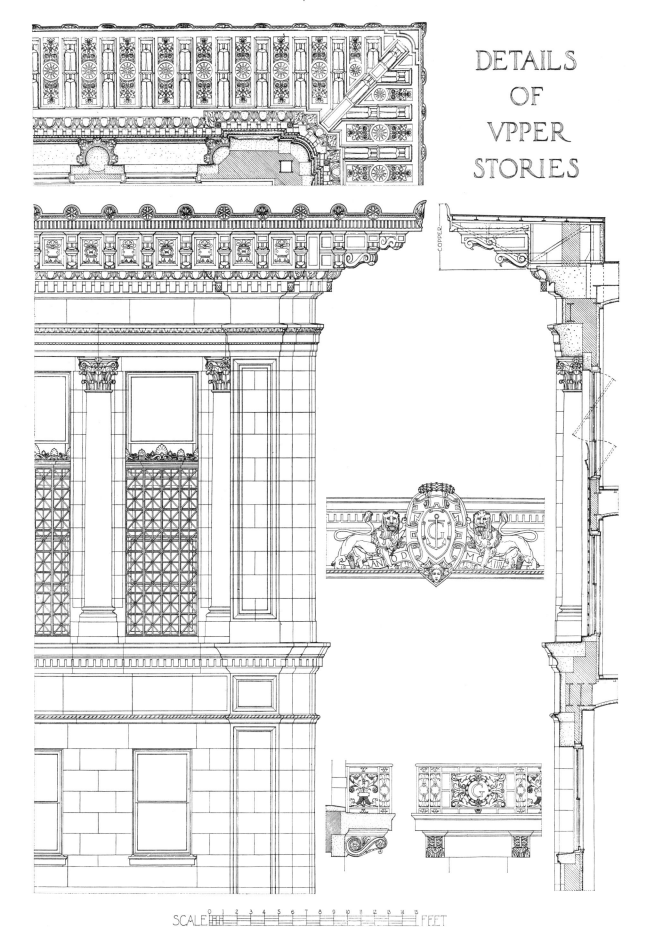

DETAILS
OF
VPPER
STORIES

SCALE FEET

DETAILS OF UPPER STORIES

BUILDING FOR THE GORHAM CO., NEW YORK CITY.

1906

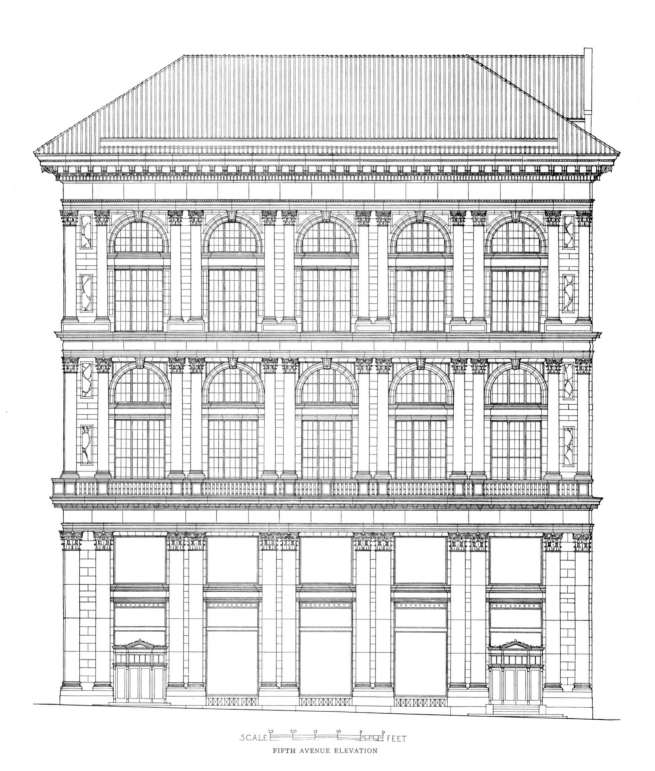

SCALE ━━━━━━ FEET

FIFTH AVENUE ELEVATION

BUILDING FOR TIFFANY & CO., NEW YORK CITY.
1906

MAIN
CORNICE

FIFTH
STORY
ORDER

THIRD STORY ORDER

SCALE ... FEET

EXTERIOR AND INTERIOR DETAILS
BUILDING FOR TIFFANY & CO., NEW YORK CITY.
1906

McKIM, MEAD & WHITE

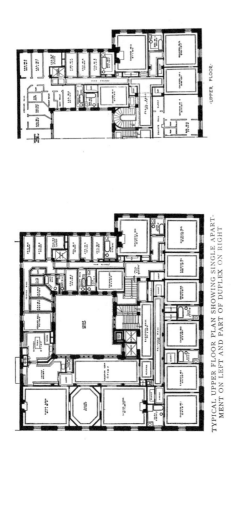

TYPICAL UPPER FLOOR PLAN SHOWING SINGLE APART-
MENT ON LEFT AND PART OF DUPLEX ON RIGHT

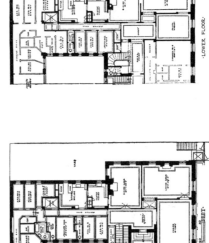

-UPPER FLOOR-

-LOWER FLOOR-

TYPICAL DUPLEX APARTMENT

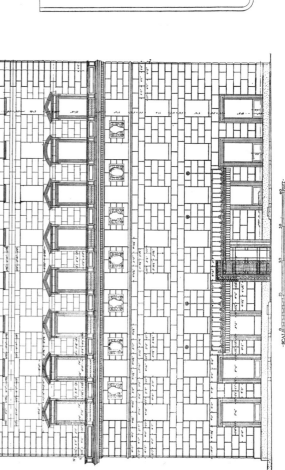

FIRST FLOOR PLAN

ELEVATION

APARTMENT HOUSE, 998 FIFTH AVENUE, FOR THE CENTURY HOLDING CO.
1911

128

McKIM, MEAD & WHITE

SCALE 0 5 10 15 20 25 30 FEET

SCALE 0 5 10 FEET

RESIDENCE OF PERCY PYNE, ESQ., NEW YORK CITY.
ABOVE, SIDE ELEVATION,   BELOW, DETAIL OF ENTRANCE, FIRST AND SECOND FLOOR PLANS
1911

129

McKIM, MEAD & WHITE

SCALE
FEET

RESIDENCE OF JOHN INNES KANE, NEW YORK CITY.
SOUTH ELEVATION
1906
130

McKIM, MEAD & WHITE

MORNING ROOM

DEN

LAVATORY

LOBBY

CLOSET

COATS

HALL

VESTIBULE

CORRT

SERVANT'S DINING ROOM

KITCHEN

SCULLERY

SERVICE HALL

GARAGE

SCALE · FOR · DETAILS·

SCALE FEET

RESIDENCE OF JOHN INNES KANE, NEW YORK CITY.
EXTERIOR DETAILS AND FIRST FLOOR PLAN
1906
131

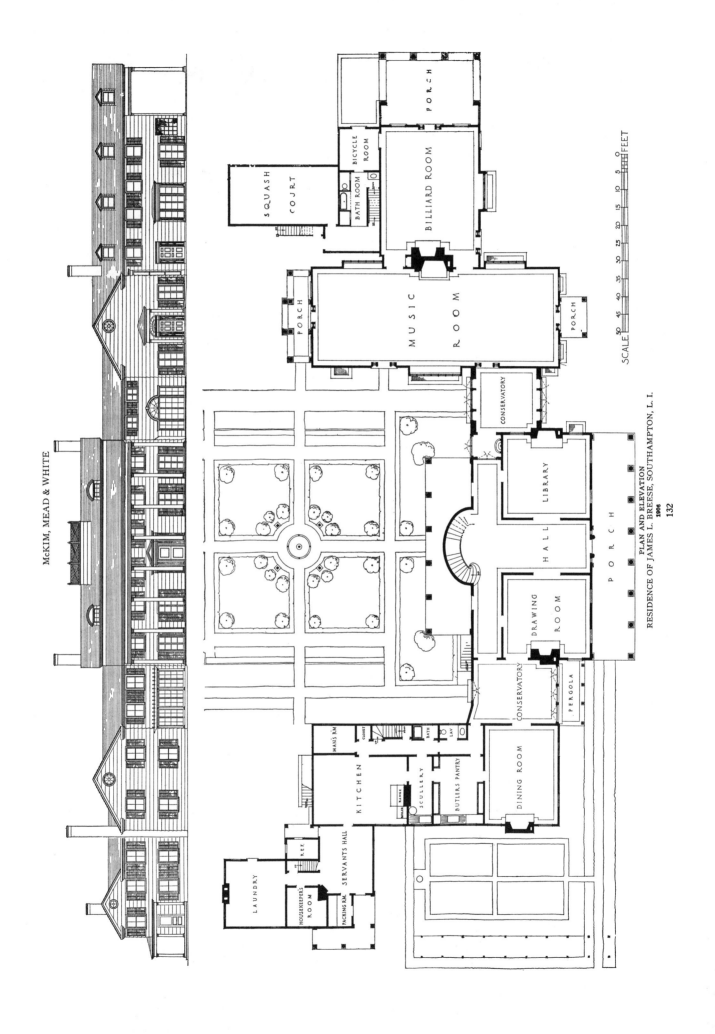

McKIM, MEAD & WHITE

SQUASH COURT

BATH ROOM

BICYCLE ROOM

PORCH

BILLIARD ROOM

PORCH

MUSIC ROOM

PORCH

CONSERVATORY

HALL

LIBRARY

PORCH

DRAWING ROOM

CONSERVATORY

PERGOLA

MAN'S RM

CLOSET

BATH

LAV.

KITCHEN

RANGE

SCULLERY

BUTLER'S PANTRY

DINING ROOM

SERVANT'S HALL

R.FR.

LAUNDRY

HOUSEKEEPER'S ROOM

PACKING RM.

SCALE

FEET

5 10 15 20 25 30 35 40 45 50

PLAN AND ELEVATION
RESIDENCE OF JAMES L. BREESE, SOUTHAMPTON, L. I.
1906

132

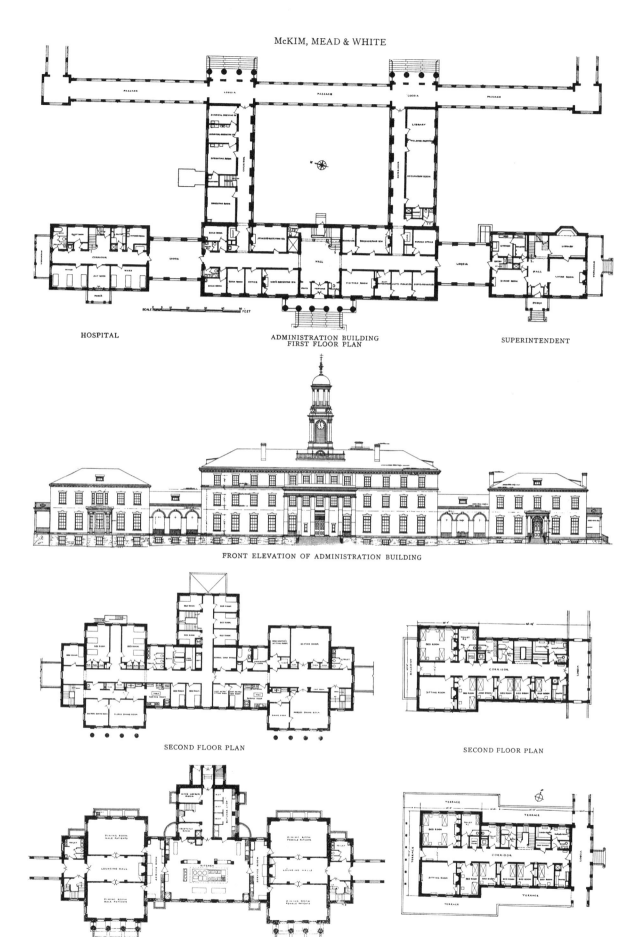

HOSPITAL

ADMINISTRATION BUILDING
FIRST FLOOR PLAN

SUPERINTENDENT

FRONT ELEVATION OF ADMINISTRATION BUILDING

SECOND FLOOR PLAN

SECOND FLOOR PLAN

FIRST FLOOR PLAN
DINING HALL BUILDING

FIRST FLOOR PLAN
TYPICAL COTTAGE

THE BURKE FOUNDATION HOSPITAL FOR CONVALESCENTS,
WHITE PLAINS, N. Y.

1914

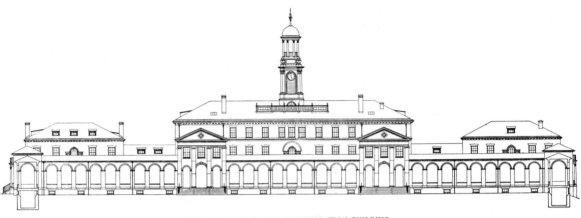

COURT ELEVATION OF ADMINISTRATION BUILDING.

COURT ELEVATION OF DINING HALL BUILDING.

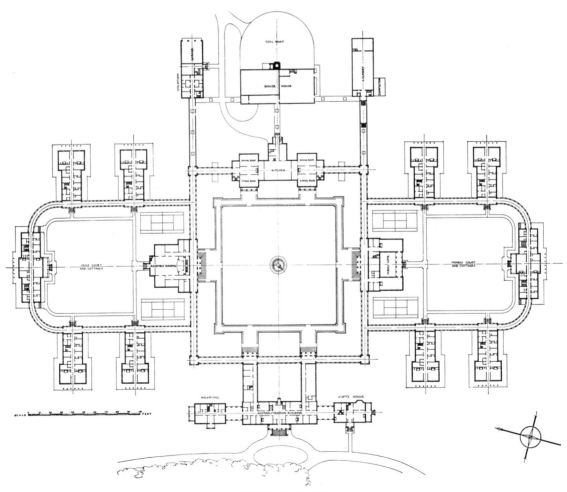

BLOCK PLAN OF GROUP
THE BURKE FOUNDATION HOSPITAL FOR CONVALESCENTS,
WHITE PLAINS, N. Y
1914

134

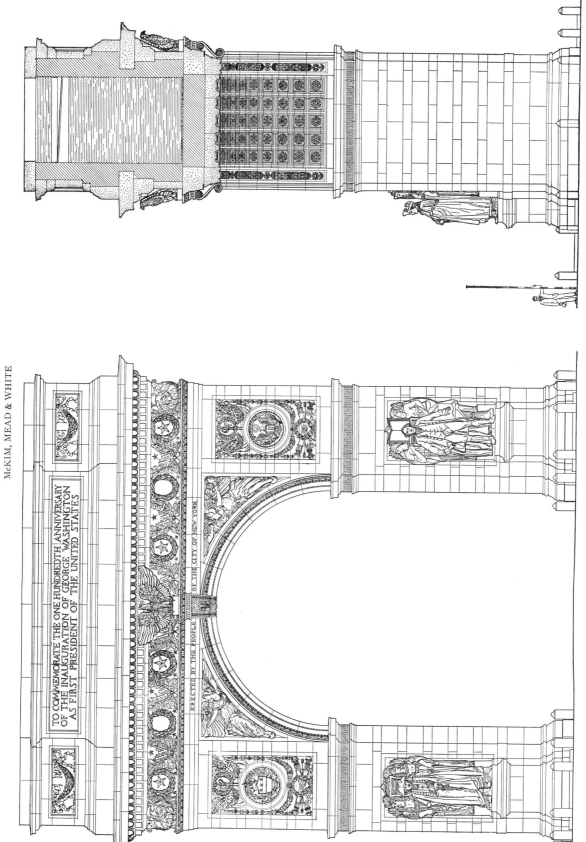

McKIM, MEAD & WHITE

TO COMMEMORATE THE ONE HUNDREDTH ANNIVERSARY
OF THE INAUGURATION OF GEORGE WASHINGTON
AS FIRST PRESIDENT OF THE UNITED STATES

ERECTED BY THE PEOPLE OF THE CITY OF NEW YORK

NORTH ELEVATION

SECTION

THE WASHINGTON ARCH, NEW YORK CITY.
1892
135

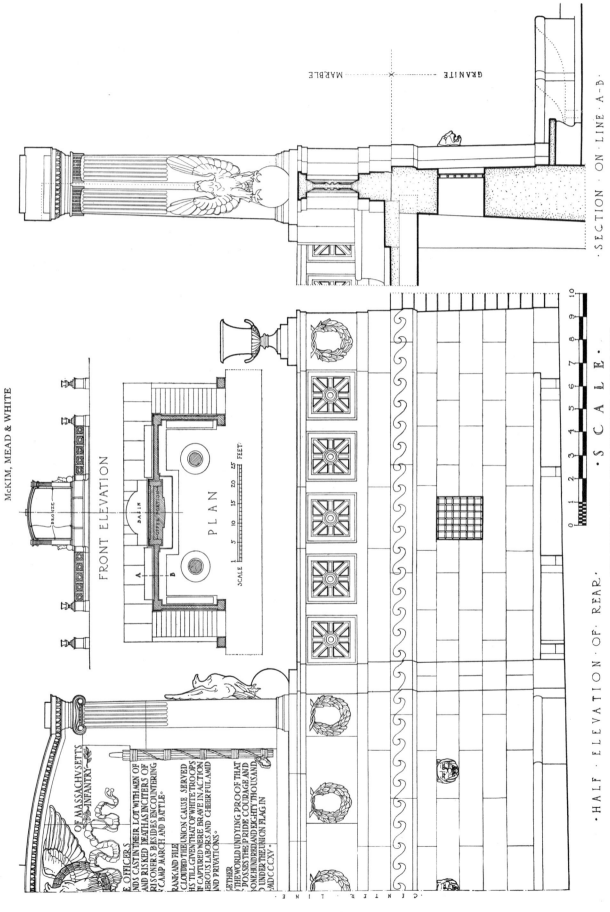

McKIM, MEAD & WHITE

FRONT ELEVATION

PLAN

SCALE 5 10 15 20 25 FEET

BRONZE

BASIN

LITTLE PORTION

A

B

· SECTION · ON · LINE · A-B ·

MARBLE

GRANITE

SCALE

0 1 2 3 4 5 6 7 8 9 10

THE ROBERT GOULD SHAW MEMORIAL, BOSTON, MASS.
1897

136

· HALF · ELEVATION · OF · REAR ·

· CENTER · LINE ·

OF MASSACHVSETTS
INFANTRY·

·E OFFICERS·
NDS CAST IN THEIR LOT WITH MEN OF
AND RISKED DEATH AS INCITERS OF
RISONERS BESIDES ENCOUNTERING
CAMP MARCH AND BATTLE·

RANK AND FILE
CLOUDED THE UNION CAUSE SERVED
HS TILL GIVEN THAT OF WHITE TROOPS
F CAPTURED WERE BRAVE IN ACTION
EROUS LABORS AND CHEERFUL AMID
ND PRIVATIONS·

GETHER
THE WORLD UNDYING PROOF THAT
POSSES THE PRIDE COURAGE AND
ONE HUNDRED AND EIGHTY THOUSAND
O UNDER THE UNION FLAG IN
MDCCCXV·